Apples
of
NEW ENGLAND

Apples
of
NEW ENGLAND

A USER'S GUIDE

Russell Steven Powell

PHOTOGRAPHS BY BAR LOIS WEEKS

The Countryman Press

Woodstock, Vermont

Interior photographs by Bar Lois Weeks
Illustration of Johnny Appleseed on page 38 courtesy of Cornell University Library, Making of America Digital Collection. It originally appeared in *Harper's New Monthly Magazine* in 1871.
Design and composition by S. E. Livingston

Published by The Countryman Press,
P.O. Box 748, Woodstock, VT 05091

Distributed by W. W. Norton & Company, Inc.,
500 Fifth Avenue, New York, NY 10110

Printed in the United States of America

10 9 8 7 6 5 4 3 2 1

Library of Congress Cataloging-in-Publication Data

Powell, Russell Steven.
  Apples of New England : a user's guide / Russell Steven Powell ; photographs by Bar Lois Weeks. — First cloth edition.
     pages cm
  Includes bibliographical references and index.
  ISBN 978-1-58157-223-0 (alk. paper)
  1. Apples—New England. 2. Apples—Varieties—New England. I. Title.

  SB363.2.U6P68 2014
  634'.11—dc23

2014015786

Contents

Introduction

There are a million ways to slice an apple. It is delicious, nutritious, artistic, sensual, culturally loaded, historically significant, a horticultural marvel, challenging to grow, and a commodity in the marketplace. It is ancient, but it is constantly reinventing itself.

There is no more democratic fruit. No food is as generous and versatile. Virtually everyone has tasted an apple; most people eat hundreds of them, fresh and cooked, use cider vinegar and other products made from apples, and imbibe gallons of its juice. Apples frequent our lives, from the McIntosh at lunch to an apple pie at Thanksgiving.

Apple trees are a distinctive feature of the New England landscape. They appear in a variety of settings: older, standard-size trees with gracious limbs and thick canopies; dwarf trees packed tightly together along long, parallel rows, harnessed to trellises; a lone, twisted tree growing wild along a stonewall; or small clusters in half-acre fields and suburban lawns.

For centuries and across cultures, from Adam and Eve to ancient Greece, apples have filled people's minds as well as their stomachs. The history of New England apples is much shorter, of course, and to date it has not produced any new myths (except for the larger-than-life figure of Massachusetts native John Chapman, better known as Johnny Appleseed). In New England, new apple varieties proliferated in the 17th, 18th, and early 19th centuries and were typically named for the town, person, or orchard where they were discovered. Many of these apples have illustrious or odd histories that have been preserved for generations. Biting into a once-popular apple discovered in New England tangibly connects us to our past. So does the enduring presence of an abandoned orchard that still produces gnarly fruit. Apples and the stories about them offer insight into more than simply diet, but also aesthetics, horticulture, weather, industrialization, and the marketplace.

Each piece of grafted fruit is a direct descendent of the original apple tree, some centuries old, for which it is named. It is hard to imagine orchards today in such urban settings as Dedham (Benoni, early 1800s), Roxbury (Roxbury Russet, 1635), or

Wilmington, Massachusetts (Baldwin, 1740), but the persistence of these varieties reminds us of those communities' agrarian roots.

Commerce and culture, rather than the orchard, are the sources of contemporary apple myths, having appropriated images of apples to symbolize innovation and style, from the Beatles' green Apple Records label in 1968 to the stylized logo of the Apple computer company in 1976 to countless interpretations of the Big Apple since it became New York City's nickname in the 1920s. Whether we eat them or not, apples are firmly in our consciousness.

Yet eating them, after all, is the main reason why we hold apples in such high esteem. No other food can be used in as many ways as apples, in so many circumstances. Apples combine sweetness with a refreshing, complex tartness, with hints of a wide range of unusual flavors: pear, citrus, pineapple, strawberries, nuts, spices, and vanilla, among others. An apple's flesh can be hard or soft, light or crunchy. Nearly all apples contain juice; some explode with it.

Apple flavor generally is at its most intense when the fruit is eaten fresh off the tree, although the flavor of certain varieties noticeably improves in storage. For weeks or months after they are picked, apples retain their flavor and crispness in a variety of ways: fresh or cooked, with other foods,

sweet or savory, served during any course of any meal on any occasion. It is no accident that colorful displays of apples are often among the first foods to greet shoppers in the grocery store. Entire cookbooks have been devoted to not just the apple, but to apple pie.

When pressed into juice, apples can be transformed into hundreds of drinks, from fresh and hard cider to brandy and ice wine, alone or blended, tasting very unlike the whole fresh apple. Similarly, apples are processed into many foods, distilled into kitchen staples, such as vinegar; dried for baking; and made into sweet foods, such as apple jelly or boiled cider.

In addition to their versatility and flavor, apples are healthy: sweet but fat free and low in calories, loaded with pectin, a good source of fiber, and full of flavonoids, phytonutrients, and antioxidants, all of which may help reduce the risk of developing cancer, hypertension, diabetes, and America's leading killer, heart disease. Apples are convenient, fitting in the hand and carried anywhere. With so many varieties and so many ways to eat and serve them, apples are a universal food, experienced by all.

The apple derives much of its cultural meaning from its rich history and because it is good to eat. But its physical beauty adds greatly to its symbolic power; Eve bites into the apple only after she has been seduced by its outer beauty, after all. Our desire for this fruit is so great, it triggers not just admiration but also lust and greed. The apple is so irresistible it becomes the perfect bait for the Witch to poison Snow White. A golden apple symbolizes the passion that led to the Trojan War.

How can a piece of fruit inspire such profound cautionary tales? Perhaps it is because we experience the apple through multiple senses: we taste its flesh, inhale its aroma, and admire its compact shape and multicolored skin. The apple is a fragrant work of art, alone or in bins, grouped with other apples, or hanging on the tree. It grows in brilliant shades of red, green, orange, and yellow, in solid colors, stripes, streaks, or patches. Some apples have intricate, meshlike patterns of russet on their skin or are completely covered in it, leaving them with a golden brown, sandpaper-like surface. An apple's skin has small pores called lenticels for respiration; on some varieties they are barely visible, but on others, white or yellow lenticels are as prominent as seeds on a strawberry. Apples are both paintings and sculpture, coming in various shapes, from slender and conical to flat and round, as big as a grapefruit or as small as a radish.

For all of its compact beauty, though, an individual apple is a mere detail, a speck in the larger canvas of the orchard. The aggregation of apple trees in an orchard creates a rare, dynamic landscape through the four seasons, beginning with spring bloom in May, when the trees flower en masse, every one covered with pink blossoms. It is a spectacular sight.

Even a few apple trees planted together command our attention. To walk through an orchard in midsummer, it is hard not to feel uplifted by the presence of thousands of pieces of healthy, maturing fruit hanging from every limb. In late fall, the leaves on many apple trees turn as brilliant as any oak or maple, and the bold, graceful gestures of leafless trees, especially the old standards, impart a rare beauty to the orchard in winter.

But it is during the fresh harvest months of September and October that the orchard hits its sensory peak. The trees and the grass beneath them are lush and green, pleasantly muffling sounds. Birds, distant tractors, or other sounds can be heard, but for the most part the orchard is a quiet place. The ripe apples on the trees are dazzling to the eye, their profusion overwhelming at times. The orchard air is perfumed, lightly scented with sweet apples, and the experience culminates in the rich, tactile pleasure of grasping an apple with one's fingers and biting into its crisp, juicy flesh.

The apple's unparalleled status as superfood, historic icon, and art object all contribute to its cultural meaning. But especially in such places as

New England, apples are also part of the fabric of the communities where they are grown. New England's apple industry, though small nationally, is incredibly diverse. People grow apples on all scales, from a few backyard trees to a hillside of heirlooms to a 10-acre pick-your own with a retail stand, to a 350-acre orchard growing apples strictly for the wholesale market. Some of our neighbors have grown apples for generations; refreshingly, despite the difficulties (including the high cost of land), some are starting out for the first time. Apples are a cash crop or a curiosity, a commodity and livelihood, depending on one's commitment and approach. For many, growing apples is a lifestyle, a demanding, 12-month job intimately connected to the natural world and its rhythms in the ancient, sacred task of growing healthy, nutritious food. In New England, many of the people who choose this life's work share the experience, inviting the general public to enjoy their privately maintained land with pick-your-owns, tours, farm stands, petting zoos and other activities, in what amounts to a public-private partnership.

New England's orchards are impossible to ignore, filling large tracts near town centers or rolling gently along rural back roads. They are constant visual reminders of human aspiration and frailty, reflecting values of perseverance, ingenuity, humility, and pride. The orchard records the human struggle to establish order out of chaos and control nature for its own ends, and nature's ultimate authority.

Aside from their eating and cultural qualities, apple trees provoke the gardener in us, inspiring our horticultural curiosity. Prolific but unpredictable from seed, apples require the unusual practice of grafting to reproduce the same variety. At times the trees are remarkably hardy, but at other times they are vulnerable and weak. They can live for two centuries or more and bear fruit throughout their lifetime, and abandoned trees can be reclaimed after years of neglect. New varieties are always being discovered, some captured by chance in nature, some developed in greenhouses and labs. Whatever we know about apples and how to grow them, there will always be more to know.

To apple lovers of all ages, may this guide serve as a useful reference point for what we know about New England apples, and for the inevitable changes to come.

1

A History of
APPLE GROWING
IN NEW ENGLAND

**Newly formed apples in late May,
soon after bloom**

Apples are practically in our DNA. They have filled our stomachs, populated our myths, and feasted our eyes since Adam and Eve.

In New England, it took less than a generation after the *Mayflower* landed at Plymouth Rock in 1620 for the first American apple variety to be discovered and named. Roxbury Russet was first recognized in what is now a Boston neighborhood in 1635 (some biographers of clergyman William Blackstone credit him with discovering a variety named Yellow Sweeting in 1623, but there are scant references to it). Whichever apple came first, it did not take long for the European settlers to reinvent the apple in the New World. Such was the importance of this versatile fruit.

Hartford, Connecticut, was the site of a 1633 apple orchard planted by Dutch traders. In Maine, orchards were planted even earlier: in 1604, on St. Croix Island, by French explorer Pierre du Gua, sieur de Monts; in the 1680s, Jean-Vincent d'Abbadie de Saint-Castin planted an orchard in the Maine town of Castine, then the capital of Acadia.

Apples were an inexpensive source of sweetness that could be enjoyed year-round in one form or another. They could be pressed into fresh cider, fermented into hard cider, or distilled into vinegar or brandy. Apples could be dried, cooked, or made into apple butter. Surplus fruit could be fed to livestock.

Apples were also familiar. The home orchard eased the early settlers' culture shock as they adjusted to a new life in New England, the trees a comforting feature of the farms and villages they left behind. Apple trees also signified ownership in the wild, new expanses of North America, and an intention to remain permanently on the land where the orchard was planted.

Initially, the English had to bring their apples with them, as there were only crab apples growing in the new country when they arrived. New England's Indians did not cultivate apples until the Jesuits arrived in the early 1600s. Even then, orchards were considered community property. Indians lived a peripatetic lifestyle, moving from food source to food source as it became available. The concept of owning land and committing to one place long enough to establish orderly rows of fruit trees was foreign to them.

As early as Blackstone in 1623, apple seeds (also called pips, pippins, or kernels) from England were already being planted in the New World, soon to be followed by young saplings or scions (cuttings) that survived the six or more weeks it typically took ships to cross the Atlantic. Once scions were grafted (implanted into rootstock) or saplings established in new soil, it was only a matter of time before English and European migrant apples mingled their genetic material with the native crab apples.

Even without the rich, new genetic material presented by the crab apples, the Old World apples would have continued to evolve, creating new, unique varieties and strains. That is what apples have done throughout history wherever they are grown. The North American crab apples, though, greatly expanded the possibilities for new and unusual fruit. They were well adapted to New England's geography and climate, increasing the likelihood that a cross between a native crab and an Old World variety would survive in its new environs.

It was not long, then, before apples began to dot the New England landscape. Wild trees from seeds discarded by farmers and scattered by birds and animals sprouted among rocks, along fences, beside roads, and on otherwise unproductive farmland. During his travels to New England in 1638 and from 1663 to 1671, Englishman John Josselyn, author of *New England Rarities Discovered* and *An Account of Two Voyages to New England*, reported seeing many apples, among other fruits, and plenty of "syder." In the latter text, he observed:

"The Countrey is replenished with fair and

AMERICA'S FIRST APPLE?

Roxbury Russet (1635) is generally accepted to be America's first named apple variety. But several biographers of Rev. William Blackstone (1595–1675) credit that distinction to him, for an apple called Yellow Sweeting (also known as Sweet Rhode Island Greening).

According to these accounts, Blackstone, also known as Blaxton, arrived in Plymouth, Massachusetts, from England in 1623, carrying a bag of apple seeds with him, which he soon planted in an orchard on Boston's Beacon Hill, on what is now the corner of Beacon and Charles Streets. The trees continued to be fruitful until the 1760s. Blackstone was an eccentric. Several accounts say that he saddled a bull and, from its back, tossed apples and flowers to his friends.

He moved to Study Hill, Rhode Island, around 1635 and planted orchards there.

There is little doubt that Blackstone planted apple trees in Boston and Rhode Island, yet few references to Yellow Sweeting can be found in any standard apple reference work. In 1765, Rhode Island governor Stephen Hopkins wrote of Blackstone, "He had the first of that sort [apples] called yellow sweetings, that were ever in this world; perhaps the richest and most delicious apple of the whole kind. Many of the trees, which he planted about one hundred and thirty years ago, are still pretty thrifty fruit bearing trees."

Dr. Everett Percy Christopher, a former dean at the University of Rhode Island (URI), wrote in 1970 that Yellow Sweeting could still be found in some old orchards in 1930, around the time Christopher began working with the state's apple growers.

URI fruit specialist Robert E. Gough shed some light on the matter in a 1978 article titled "Apples from Rhode Island." Gough confirms Blackstone's discovery of Yellow Sweeting, and he cites a 1950 reference from botanist Ulysses P. Hedrick, which states it was used primarily as a rootstock for grafts from other varieties "because of the hardiness and vigor."

By Gough's time, though, the variety was virtually unknown. He lists its tree and fruit characteristics as "uncertain," and its availability as "unknown."

large Orchards. It was affirmed by one Mr. Wool-cut (a magistrate in Connecticut Colony) at the Captains Messe (of which I was) aboard the Ship I came home in, that he made Five hundred Hogsheads of Syder out of his own Orchard in one year. Syder is very plentiful in the Countrey."

By 1720, there was "a well defined Indian path [now a part of the Appalachian National Scenic Trail] leading from the Stockbridge tribe along the valley of the Housatonic, through Weatogue, to the Scaticoke settlement at Kent, Connecticut," reported Judge Church of Great Barrington, Massachusetts, where "apple trees had sprung up, and were growing along that path through its whole extent, at unequal distances, accurately enough marking its course."

In addition to these wild trees, the early settlers experimented with grafted apples in many environments, even on the beach. In 1653 Thomas Rogers planted "Garden by the Sea," an apple orchard along the southern Maine coast in what is now Old Orchard Beach. Rogers was forced to flee from Indians in 1675, eventually resettling in Kittery, Maine, 40 miles south, but the abandoned orchard endured for more than 150 years. Two centuries after Rogers planted his orchard, Henry David Thoreau in his book *Cape Cod* related his impressions of the strange, gnarly, low-growing apple trees he encountered during three hikes along the Atlantic on the eastern edge of Massachusetts between 1849 and 1855.

Apples had friends in high places in colonial New England. John Endecott (1588–1665), first governor of Massachusetts Bay Colony, placed an order for apple seeds from England in 1629. The trees from these seeds grew well, but in 1644, Endecott experienced a setback. "My children," he wrote to his successor, Governor John Winthrop (1588–1649), "burnt mee at least 500 trees this spring by setting the ground on fire neere them." Fortunately for Endecott, the orchard recovered quickly, and by 1648 he was able to trade 500 three-year-old apple saplings to Captain William W. Trask, one of the founders of Massachusetts Bay Colony, for 200 acres of land.

Gov. Winthrop traded in apples, too. He was granted rights to Conant's Island in Boston Harbor by the Massachusetts General Court in 1632, and he renamed it Governor's Garden. In exchange, Winthrop agreed to plant an orchard and a vineyard there, and to pay one-fifth of his annual income to the sitting governor, whoever he might be. The court amended his rent in 1634 to "a hogshead of the best wyne that shall grow there to be paide yearly, after the death of the said John Winthrop and noething before."

Several years later, the rent was changed again, to "two bushels of apples every yeare one bushel to the Governour & another to the General Court in winter,—the same to bee of the best apples there growing." The General Court records of 1640 report that "Mr. Winthrop, Senior, paid in his bushel of apples."

Apples were a valued commodity and added to property values. In 1648, John Balch of Beverly, Massachusetts, left his widow half of "the great fruit trees," with the other half left to his eldest son. A younger son received younger trees.

The first tree nursery in New England was started by George Fenwick of Saybrook, Connecticut, in 1641. Henry Wolcott Jr. operated a nursery in Connecticut in 1648, but closed five years later so he could concentrate on growing apples for cider. There is no clear record when apple varieties were first grafted in New England, but in a 1772 advertisement in *Boston News-Letter*, Sarah Dawson "widow of Joseph Dawson, Gardner, in Cambridge Street, at the Cold Bath,—has got, a large Collection of grafted and inoculated English Fruit-Trees of all sorts where Gentlemen may have their Choice among three or four hundred which will be ready to be removed this Fall."

Most early orchards were small, though, part of diverse farms and household gardens meant to be self-sustaining, with a mix of fruits, vegetables, and animals: a few chickens for eggs, cows for milk, sheep for wool, pigs for meat. The early settlers also grew such crops as flax and wheat. A few apple trees enhanced their diet and completed the landscape.

For their main uses in cooking and in cider, apples did not have to be sweet, or even edible. The juice from almost any apple becomes palatable when pressed into cider, especially when blended with other varieties. A sour or bitter apple can be transformed in cooking, especially if fortified by spices; sweeteners, such as honey or molasses; or other ingredients or fruit. When an apple was discovered that was good eaten fresh, it was a bonus. If the apple stored well, people could be somewhat forgiving of an unattractive skin or a bland flavor.

When a farmer discovered a chance seedling that produced edible fruit, he took scions from it for grafting in his home orchard. Perhaps he gave or sold some to his neighbors, friends, and relatives. In this way a variety was born, typically named for the place or the person who discovered it.

Some of these early varieties survive today, but most of them eventually lost favor with growers and the public, supplanted by newer apples with superior flavor, looks, or storage capabilities, that were easier to grow, bore bigger, more reliable crops, or shipped well. Perhaps the particular soil and microclimate that produced an outstanding apple could not be replicated elsewhere.

Massachusetts native John Chapman ("Johnny

Appleseed") is well known for planting apple seeds along the western frontier in Ohio and Indiana between 1806 and 1845. But he was not the only New Englander to spread the apple gene. David Church of Newington, Connecticut, reporting on his travels to New York State in 1810, wrote, "I have been carrying out appleseeds . . . little by little till I have carried out thirteen bushel and a half and put them in eighty nurseries and have got a hundred thousand trees I suppose."

By the beginning of the 19th century in New England, though, newly discovered apples from chance seedlings were supplemented with an increasing number of named, grafted varieties from Europe and beyond, many of them good for fresh eating. Apple growers sold their fruit locally and planted varieties that allowed them to extend the fresh harvest as far as possible. Early- and late-season varieties, and apples that remained firm and flavorful through the winter were in high demand.

APPLE GROWERS AND ABOLITIONISTS

Two of the most influential champions of the apple in the 19th century were John Kenrick (1755–1833) and his son William (1789–1872) of Newton, Massachusetts. For decades they operated Nonantum Hill, the leading plant and fruit tree nursery in New England.

The two men did more than grow and sell fruit, though. John Kenrick discovered a variety named Kenrick (also known as Kenrick's Red Autumn), a juicy, sweet-tart, green-skinned apple covered in red. William Kenrick wrote two influential books on horticulture: *The New American Orchardist* (1833), which went through seven editions, and *The American Silk Grower's Guide* (1835), during New England's flirtation with silk culture and mulberry trees.

Father and son had something else in common besides apples and genes: they were both outspoken abolitionists.

In 1775, John Kenrick acquired the land on which he later established his nursery, on the southwestern slope of Newton's Nonantum Hill. He planted peaches in 1790, and four years later opened the nursery, offering a wide selection of fruit trees and bushes. Over the next decade he added ornamental trees, including two acres of Lombardy poplars (then in high demand), and many varieties of berries and tree fruit imported from Europe.

John Kenrick took a public stand in 1817 when he published a 59-page booklet entitled *The Horrors of Slavery,* which strongly criticized American society for sustaining the institution of slavery. At the time his booklet appeared, Kenrick's position

Nurserymen, such as John Kenrick of Newton, Massachusetts, stepped up to meet this need. Kenrick started Nonantum Hill Nursery in 1794, and eventually it became the largest in the region; at its peak in the 1830s it offered more than 200 varieties of apples. Ephraim Goodale offered 10 varieties of apples at a nursery in Buckport, Maine, around 1800. Deacon Daniel P. Dyer established a major nursery in Pocasset, Rhode Island, near Providence, in 1824, while Moore's Nursery in Providence listed more than 100 varieties of apple tree in the 1840s, leading to many new or expanded orchards in Rhode Island between 1825 and 1860. The nurseries also supplied growers in much of New England and New York State.

Despite the availability of a wide range of English, French, and German "dessert" varieties, though, apples were still valued more for cooking and cider than for fresh eating. From colonial times until the mid-1800s, fresh or hard cider was controversial; most Northerners viewed slavery as a regional issue for individual states to decide. Kenrick's nursery continued to thrive, though, and in 1823 *New England Farmer,* the leading agricultural newspaper of the time, described it as "the finest in America."

By the early 1830s, William, John's eldest son, had established a separate business on adjoining land, and when John died in 1833, William brought the two nurseries together. Through his writing and other activities he became an even more influential horticulturalist than his father. A founding member of the Massachusetts Horticultural Society, William Kenrick sat on its governing council from 1829 to 1841, and for many years served on its standing committee on fruit trees and fruit.

William Kenrick sold a tremendous variety of fruit-bearing trees at Nonantum Hill. His first catalog in 1832 lists 148 varieties of apples, 155 pears, 99 peaches, 48 cherries, and 47 plums. By 1838, the number of apple varieties had risen to 228, and 317 pears.

William Kenrick's activities were not limited to horticulture any more than his father's were. He articulated his uncompromising anti-slavery views in a series of letters to his friend Horace Mann, a US representative, also of Newton, during the North-South crisis of 1849–50.

William Kenrick retired in 1856, but the Nonantum Hill nursery continued to be operated by his brother, John A. Kenrick, under the name Nonantum Dale Gardens.

was America's main beverage. Hard cider was inexpensive and easy to make, it could be stored year-round, and it aged to a pleasant, slightly fizzy, lightly alcoholic drink.

Cider was sweet, mildly intoxicating, and in some places, safer to drink than water. Everyone drank hard cider, even children and the elderly. Middlesex County, Massachusetts, produced 33,436 barrels of cider in 1764, "or seven per family, well over a barrel for every man, woman, and child." Farmers stored up to 50 barrels, enough to last a year. The cider was served freely to all house guests: travelers, friends, and neighbors, even peddlers and Indians.

Maine settlers from Massachusetts brought apple seeds with them. One of the largest seedling orchards around 1770 was planted by Ichabod Howe, who had moved to Winthrop, Maine, from Ipswich, Massachusetts. Several of his trees became named varieties, and Howe made the first cider in Winthrop, according to Ulysses P. Hedrick, "by crushing the apples in a sap trough and pressing out the juice in a cheese press."

Dutch immigrant John Linklaen spoke of "superb orchards" in Vermont's Connecticut River Valley soon after his arrival in America in 1791. East of the river in Walpole, New Hampshire, John Bellow grew 30 acres of apples in 1805 and made 4,800 42-gallon barrels of cider, or more than 200,000 gallons. Assuming about 30 trees per acre, he would have harvested more than 60 bushels of apples per tree to produce this total. At the beginning of the 19th century there were good-size orchards from Worcester County, Massachusetts, to western Connecticut, where small towns, such as Woodbury, had "many valuable orchards, so that the making of cider and cider spirits are important agricultural interests," according to one report.

From cider, apples could be distilled into brandy, or applejack, a much stronger drink, and it was widely produced around this time. Torrington, Connecticut, had four cider mills and one brandy still in 1774. Berkshire and Hampshire counties in western Massachusetts produced 265,000 gallons of brandy in 1810. There were as many as 10 distillers of applejack in Newtown, Connecticut, eight in Canton.

By the mid-1800s, though, hard cider's dominance began to fade, the target of temperance movements at either end of the century, and supplanted by an inexpensive urban alternative, beer.

Local temperance societies appeared in Litchfield, Connecticut, in 1787, and Adams, Massachusetts, in 1792. In 1813, the Massachusetts Society for the Suppression of Intemperance was established in Boston. Thirteen years later, a national campaign against alcohol began in Boston with the formation of the American Temperance

Society. In less than a decade, it grew to more than 8,000 chapters across the country, and more than 1,500,000 members. As a widely used—and abused—drink, hard cider became a symbol of alcohol's evils, and consumption fell.

By midcentury hard cider faced increased competition from beer. New England's rural population was flocking to its cities and mill towns in search of work, and living among new immigrant populations from such countries as Germany, bringing with them a talent for brewing beer. Urbanization did not singlehandedly ruin the market for cider, but it played a big part.

The final blow to the hard cider market came in the form of a second temperance movement that began with the creation of the Woman's Christian Temperance Union in 1874. Despite the movement, in 1900 Americans still drank an estimated 55 million gallons of hard cider. But that figure dropped to 13 million gallons in 1919 after passage of the Volstead Act, the enabling legislation for the 18th Amendment to the United States Constitution, which established National Prohibition of alcoholic beverages. Even after Prohibition ended in 1933, the market for hard cider never recovered.

Despite this, the New England apple industry grew dramatically during the 1800s, as its apples were in demand in other, more lucrative markets. New England shipped many of its apples to export markets in such countries as England and in the West Indies. England became a huge market for New England apples. In 1896 nearly one million barrels were shipped to England from Boston, mostly Baldwins, Roxbury Russets, and Rhode Island Greenings. Steamers with Maine apples left Portland for England every week.

The apples were shipped in sealed wooden barrels with the grower's name and variety on top, inked through a metal stencil. Each barrel held 2 3/4 bushels, or 100 quarts, of apples, and required careful hand packing. "Many a sale of good fruit has been spoiled by poor packing," Vermont pomologist Frank A. Waugh wrote in 1908. "When fruit is to be shipped some distance, as across the ocean, the packing must be irreproachable." The standard American 100-quart barrel had a diameter at the top and bottom of 17 1/2 inches, widening to a diameter of 20 3/8 inches in the middle (with a circumference of 64 inches), and staves that were 28 1/2 inches long. A flatter, more cylindrical "Nova Scotia" barrel held 96 quarts but rocked less during shipping, so it was preferred for exports.

Domestically, growers gradually turned to packing their apples in bushel-size wooden boxes. The boxes were sturdier than baskets and easier to move and display than the larger barrels. They are still in use at many orchards today, although

FROM RUSSIA TO NEW ENGLAND

Russian apple varieties were much sought after in 19th-century New England for their hardiness in cold climates. Russian varieties Alexander, Duchess of Oldenburg, Red Astrachan, and Tetofsky were imported by the Massachusetts Horticultural Society between 1830 and 1835.

Physician and writer Dr. Thomas H. Hoskins (1828–1902) began growing apples after relocating from Boston to Newport, Vermont, and soon began introducing new, hardy varieties to New England, including McIntosh from Canada, Wealthy from Minnesota, and several Russian apples.

A native of Gardiner, Maine, Hoskins graduated from Louisville [Kentucky] Medical School in 1866. He began his career as a physician and surgeon in the Boston area until a severe spinal injury from a fall on ice incapacitated him. He moved to Newport, a small town near the Canadian border along the southern end of Lake Memphremagog, to recuperate, and decided it would be a good place to grow fruit.

Hoskins established a nursery in nearby West Derby around 1868 and began experimenting with apple varieties. He bought a farm in Newport Center, where he planted a 12-acre orchard, and in 1890 he purchased 135 acres in Derby and developed one of the best orchards in New England at the time, with nearly 100 varieties of apple trees.

Hoskins is credited with planting the first McIntosh sapling in the United States, purchased in 1868 from the John McIntosh family nursery in Dun-

they have been replaced with lighter, cheaper, corrugated cardboard boxes for shipping.

By the 1930s, packinghouses were becoming more and more mechanized as growers sought to develop uniform grades and standards. But much of the grading and sorting was still done by hand. At such orchards as Elm Hill Farm in Brookfield, Massachusetts, and Brookdale Farm in Hollis, New Hampshire, apples were individually wrapped in tissue paper with the farm's name and logo on it before being placed in a box. While labor intensive, it protected the apples from bruising and made an attractive presentation. "You got pretty fast at it," recalls Eleanor Whittemore of Brookdale, demonstrating the act by swiping an imaginary tissue from a box with her left hand and bringing it swiftly together with an apple in her right hand, wrapping the apple in a single motion and then reaching for the next.

Apples remained in high demand domestically for such products as vinegar, and by processors for canning or drying for hotels, grocery stores, and

dela, Ontario. He brought to general notice a local apple from Newport, Scott Winter, in 1864. Hoskins continually searched for apple varieties that could withstand Newport's cold climate, and through his efforts he introduced several Russian apples to New England and the United States. The apples (and their Russian names) included Cut Wine, also known as Wine Rubets (Vinograd), Golden White (Beel Solotofskaja), Prolific Sweeting (Plodowitka Cuadkaja), Russian Baldwin, St. Peter, Yellow Calville (Voronesh No. 21), and Yellow Transparent (Skwosnoi Schotoi).

Hoskins also had a distinguished career as a writer on food and agriculture. During his years as a physician in the Boston area, he worked as an editorial writer for the *Boston Courier,* and authored a pamphlet, "A Treatise on the Adulteration of Food." In Vermont, he served as agricultural editor of the *Newport Express.* For two decades Hoskins was agricultural editor of the *Vermont Watchman and State Journal* and *Vermont Watchman,* and he was a regular contributor to *Rural New Yorker, Garden and Forest, American Gardening,* and other journals.

In 1870 Hoskins cofounded and edited *The Vermont Farmer,* which described itself as "an agricultural and family newspaper for the ruralists of the Green Mountain State." After two years in Newport, publisher Royal Cummings and Hoskins moved operations south to St. Johnsbury, where he continued to serve as editor for the next two years. The periodical reached a peak circulation in 1875 of just over 3,600.

export. From 1920 to 1950, about seven million bushels of apples were dried annually. The fishing fleet in Gloucester, Massachusetts, used 37 tons of dried apples in a year to make pies and applesauce for its 4,300 fishermen.

Canned apples, mostly in large containers for use by bakeries and large institutions, rose from four million bushels in 1920 to nearly ten million bushels in 1950. Frozen apples became popular during World War II due to a shortage of tin for cans.

Most of New England's apple crop had to be preserved or processed to make it last more than a few weeks after harvest. Out of season, until the late 1800s fresh apples were stored in various ways, with varying degrees of success: in piles in the orchard, buried in pits or covered by hay, put in bins in cellars or spread out on attic floors. Some of these methods lacked merit altogether, and the best were only marginally effective. Drying was a good way for a farm family to preserve a year-round supply of apples, and the dried fruit was especially good in pies. But the work of slicing apples into quarters and placing them on boards or hanging them from string to dry was tedious.

New England farmers became better organized and began taking a more professional, scientific approach to agriculture in the 1860s with the establishment of land grant universities and agricultural experiment stations in all six states. Horticultural societies were formed in Massachusetts in 1829, Worcester County in 1842, Rhode Island in 1845, Connecticut in 1887, and Vermont in 1896, to introduce new varieties to the region and "encourage the science and practice of horticulture." Apple growers formed the Maine State Pomological Society in 1873, the Connecticut Pomological Society in 1891, and statewide fruit grower associations in Massachusetts (1895) and Rhode Island (1913).

It took until the 1860s for growers to associate disease to apples and trees with insects or bacteria. Prior to that, if trees failed or fruit was spoiled, it was assumed to be the result of inadequate soils, improper planting, or poor cultivation. In *Two Voyages to New England*, John Josselyn, referring to cherry trees, took a decidedly unscientific view of disease:

"Their fruit trees are subject to two diseases, the Meazels, which is when they are burned and scotched with the sun, and Lowziness, when the woodpeckers jab holes in their bark; the way to cure them when they are lowzie is to bore a hole in the main trunk with an augur, and pour in a quantity of Brandie or Rhum, and then stop it up with a pin made of the same tree."

From the 1860s on, treatment of orchard pests became more sophisticated, although spraying trees with pesticides did not become a general practice until the early 1900s. For most of the 1800s, many New England farms had small orchards, from as few as several trees to one or two acres. Trees did not generally receive specialized care, and they were only fertilized occasionally with barnyard manure. There were no severe insect and disease problems, and spraying was an unknown practice. It was expected that most apples in the marketplace would have some blemishes.

Most orchards had livestock grazing in them, which kept the grass down. Growers later used hand scythes to clear away grass beneath trees. In Maine, saplings were "pruned up" to a height of 5 to 6 feet before they were allowed to branch, wrote Clarence Albert Day in *A History of Maine Agriculture, 1604–1860*, "to accommodate mowing, plowing and planting among them and to prevent sheep from picking apples and browsing on the lower limbs."

Three of the most commonly grown apples in the United States in the 1700s and 1800s were discovered in New England: Sheep's Nose, Roxbury Russet, and Westfield-Seek-No-Further. Sheep's Nose was considered the best baking apple, and it was better known than any other apple. Wherever settlers traveled from Connecticut, they took Sheep's Nose with them. Roxbury Russet, being a good storage apple, was highly valued. Westfield-Seek-No-Further was prized as a cider and fresh-eating apple.

With growing markets and increased education and support, New England's apple industry was thriving at the dawn of the 20th century. Massachusetts doubled its production between 1890 and 1900. Maine had more than four million of New England's approximately 11 million bearing apple trees in 1900. Even tiny Rhode Island had a good-size crop.

In the late 1800s, nearly all of Grand Isle County, Vermont's 50,000 acres were in agriculture. By 2007, only about one-third of the county's acreage was still farmed, with just 201 acres in apples. The state's smallest county comprises several north–south, interconnected islands in the center of Lake Champlain. The population of its five towns (Alburgh, Grand Isle, Isle La Motte, North Hero, and South Hero) in 1900 was about 4,500, compared to about 7,000 residents in 2010.

Despite its small size, Grand Isle County has been an important apple-growing region of Vermont for more than a century. Surrounded by the temperate waters of Lake Champlain, the islands have been a good place for growing apples. Grand Isle County orchards harvested a large crop of 40,424 barrels of marketable apples in 1896, mostly Northern Spy, Rhode Island Greening, Baldwin, Fameuse, Tolman's Sweet, Pound Sweet, Golden Russet, Ben Davis, Yellow Bellflower, and Arctic.

Vermont's largest apple-growing region volume-wise ran parallel to Grand Isle County on land east of the islands. The Champlain Valley, sandwiched between Lake Champlain's eastern shore and the Green Mountains, stretches south from Burlington in northern Vermont to the center of the state in Middlebury. The area has been known for its apple production since the 1850s, when the leading apple-growing towns were Brandon, Burlington, Vergennes, Bennington, Middlebury, and Cornwall. The Champlain Valley orchards grew many of the same varieties as Grand Isle, plus Esopus Spitzenburg, King of Tompkins County, Red Astrachan, Westfield Seek-No-Further, Roxbury Russet, Chenango Strawberry, Hubbardston Nonesuch, and Gravenstein.

As more and better American varieties were developed and with advances in storage and horticulture, apples were increasingly marketed for fresh eating. Apple growing was becoming more specialized and sophisticated. With the widespread availability of refrigeration by 1900, growers could plant fewer varieties and harvest them more efficiently, and store and ship apples more effectively than ever before. This expansion in capacity in turn led to an increase in larger, commercial orchards (and a decrease in small farm orchards).

Armed with new methods, new markets, new varieties, and facing declining demand for cider, New England's growers were well on the way to rebranding the apple from a mainly cooking and processing fruit to one for fresh eating. In 1904 at the St. Louis World's Fair, horticulturist J. T. Stinson introduced the phrase "An apple a day keeps the doctor away," an updated version of a Welsh proverb, and it became the national slogan for the new era.

Longtime New England stalwarts Baldwin, Northern Spy, and Rhode Island Greening were the most widely grown apples in the Northeast at the time. All three varieties were widely praised. In *The Fruits of America* (1852), Charles Ma-

TWO HOMES FOR ONE APPLE

Both Connecticut and New York claim Northern Spy as their own, because the trees that produced the first Northern Spy apples were grown in East Bloomfield, New York, from seeds brought there from Salisbury, Connecticut.

Heman Chapin (1770–1843) left Salisbury in 1796 for a 400-acre farm in East Bloomfield where he grew, sold, and shipped apples, grapes, and other fruits with his son, Oliver C. Chapin.

Remarkably, three named apple varieties emerged from seeds Chapin brought with him from Connecticut to New York. Two of these, Early Joe (1843), a small, early-season apple with red stripes, and Melon (released in 1845), a large, late-season red apple, survive as little-grown heirlooms.

Northern Spy is by far the most successful of the three. One of the most widely grown apples in the Northeast in the late 19th and early 20th centuries, it is still grown commercially, mostly for processing, in parts of New York and Michigan. While it can be somewhat hard to find in New England, it is enjoying a modest comeback for its qualities as a fresh eating apple, for baking (especially in pies), and in fresh and hard cider.

The first Northern Spy apples did not come directly from the Salisbury seeds. The original tree died before it could bear fruit, but Chapin's brother-in-law, Roswell Humphrey, made grafts from it and raised the first Northern Spy apples, introducing them in 1840.

son Hovey called Rhode Island Greening "unsurpassed" as a cooking apple, "and as a dessert fruit of its season, has few equals." An article in *New England Farmer* in 1885 said of Baldwin, "What the Concord is among grapes, what the Bartlett has been among pears, the Baldwin is among apples." Spencer A. Beach, in *The Apples of New York* (1905) wrote that Northern Spy "is superior to either of these in flavor and quality."

Yet all three apples were approaching their commercial peak, beset with horticultural problems and unable to compete with newer, hardier varieties, such as McIntosh from Canada (1870) and Cortland from New York (1898).

Discovered in Wilmington, Massachusetts, in 1740, Baldwin was New England's most popular apple for nearly two centuries before succumbing to a deep freeze in the winter of 1933/34. Baldwin's eventual demise can be traced to its lack of hardiness, but it may also have become a victim of its own success. Although he still recommended it for planting in every New England state, in 1908 Frank A. Waugh described Baldwin as "exactly the apple for the ordinary man. It is an ordinary apple."

Rhode Island Greening is even older than Baldwin, dating back to the 1600s. It was especially popular in New York State—Rhode Island Greening and Baldwin together accounted for two-thirds of the New York crop in 1900—but began to lose market share due to its susceptibility to storage scald, a condition following cold storage which leaves brown patches of dead cells on and sometimes just beneath the apple's peel, compromising its keeping qualities (Baldwin is also susceptible to scald).

Northern Spy, grown in East Bloomfield, New York, from seeds from Salisbury, Connecticut, was introduced in 1840. While an outstanding, all-purpose apple, Northern Spy, too, had fatal commercial flaws. It took Northern Spy trees several more years to begin bearing fruit than most varieties. It was not known for producing large crops, and it could be difficult to grow. Yet because of what Waugh called the apple's "unsurpassed quality," Northern Spy still returned high prices in the early 1900s, and it was widely grown in Maine, Massachusetts, New Hampshire, and Vermont.

With the advent of refrigeration, russeted apples, with their naturally rough, brownish skins, known for their outstanding storage qualities as well as their flavor, were already losing market share. Most of the russeted apples were small to medium in size, and consumers wanted larger apples for cooking. By 1900, New England's most popular russets, Roxbury and Golden, were mostly exported to England via Nova Scotia.

Now that apples could be stored longer and shipped further than ever before, the 18th- and

19th-century emphasis on many varieties to extend the season was shifting to a new, more specialized approach. "The fruit grower may confront himself—as mostly he does—with the knowledge that he is not required to know or identify many varieties," Waugh wrote. "If he is a strictly up-to-date grower he will cultivate only half a dozen varieties, or even less. These he must know perfectly. He must know all their smallest points—their ins and outs—their weaknesses and idiosyncrasies—as he knows the members of his own family. But other varieties have only a general and distant interest for him."

Apple growing for market, he wrote, required just a few standard varieties "and the dismissal of all others, even of the choicest family favorites."

Yet in 1900, most apples postharvest were still kept in well-ventilated, heavily insulated buildings or rooms, known as common storage, rather than refrigerated. T. L. Kinney of South Hero, Vermont, for example, added a 30-foot by 50-foot common storage room in 1888. Charles L. Green of East Wilton, Maine, built a 30- by 40-foot common storage room in 1903. Both Kinney's and Green's buildings stored up to 2,000 barrels divided equally between their cellars and main floors, with room for 1,000 or more empty barrels in the attic. Only gradually were these buildings retrofitted or replaced with refrigeration, or "cold storage." The first dedicated cold storage in Maine was built in the early 1920s by Everett Sturtevant of Winthrop.

By 1930, commercial orchards of 100 or more trees accounted for more than half of New England's apple crop, produced by nearly six million bearing trees in 1925. Maine was the leading state, with more than 2.4 million trees producing one million barrels of apples annually, followed by Massachusetts (1.4 million trees), Connecticut (700,000 trees), New Hampshire (620,000 trees), Vermont (559,000 trees), and Rhode Island (166,000 trees). Nearly two million additional trees in New England's orchards had not yet begun bearing fruit, but the region's apple industry still had declined from its peak of 11 million bearing trees in 1900, largely as a result of the loss of many small farm orchards. The biggest decreases in the number of apple trees were in Maine, New Hampshire, and Vermont, which fell by 40 percent between 1910 and 1930, although losses in production were somewhat offset by the increased yields of commercial orchards. This followed a national trend, as the number of apple trees in the United States declined 36 percent between 1910 and 1925, from 217 million to 138 million trees.

Baldwin production peaked in New England between 1910 and 1920, but in 1930 it still com-

THE SHOREHAM CO-OP EXPERIMENT

An innovative cooperative of Vermont apple growers was formed just after World War II and thrived for more than half a century. The Shoreham Cooperative Apple Producers Association (SCAPA) consisted of four Champlain Valley growers and one sales agent when it began construction of a storage warehouse in 1946. From this modest beginning until its peak in 1986, the warehouse's capacity grew more than tenfold, from 40,000 bushels to 500,000 bushels, or about half of Vermont's total production, with 26 member growers.

SCAPA built the first controlled atmosphere (CA) storage in New England in 1951; its first CA room had a capacity of 11,000 bushels. By 1978, the warehouse could store 240,000 bushels in CA and 50,000 bushels in regular cold storage, and another 50,000 bushels were packed out fresh each fall. In 1984, the co-op had 18 CA rooms and four regular cold storage rooms from 23 members who produced more than 450,000 bushels of mostly McIntosh, Red Delicious, Golden Delicious, Empire, Cortland, Northern Spy, Rome, Rhode Island Greening, and Idared. Its apples were sold all over the world.

But at the beginning of the 1990s, the New England apple industry was under stress from factors ranging from the Alar scandal in 1989, to Hurricane Bob in 1991, to increased competition from Washington State. The co-op's largest grower, Cornwall Orchards, was forced to close in the early 1990s, taking with it nearly half of SCAPA's apples. The co-op never recovered, and unable to make needed repairs to the warehouse, it went out of business in 2002.

At the time SCAPA folded, Sunrise Orchards in Cornwall was its largest grower, and it still needed storage space for its crop. In 2004, Sunrise owners Christiana and Barney Hodges Jr. teamed with Gregory O'Brien to purchase two-thirds of the original warehouse (Seedway purchased the remaining third), and they formed a new company, Vermont Refrigerated Storage.

Since then, the new owners have invested in repairs to the building. In 2014 Vermont Refrigerated Storage stored apples for Sunrise, Crescent, and Champlain Orchards in Vermont, and Gunnison, Northern, and Apple Hill Orchards in New York, with capacity to spare.

prised nearly 40 percent of the New England crop, followed distantly by McIntosh, which had been planted extensively since about 1910 and was rapidly gaining market share, and then Red Delicious, Wealthy, and Gravenstein. Rhode Island Greening and Northern Spy completed the "New England Seven," although the region's agricultural extension agents considered Baldwin, Gravenstein, and Rhode Island Greening "unwise" for Vermont, recommending hardier varieties, such as Cortland and Fameuse, instead.

By the late 1940s, Massachusetts had become the region's leading producer (now measured in 42-pound bushel boxes rather than by number of trees, or by 2 3/4-bushel barrels), averaging almost 2.5 million bushels annually from 1938 to 1948. Connecticut was next, averaging more than 1.2 million bushels, followed by Maine and New Hampshire (about 720,000 bushels each), Vermont (626,000 bushels), and Rhode Island (218,000 bushels). McIntosh by the mid-1940s had become the dominant variety throughout New England, with three times the production of Baldwin. Cortland was beginning to pass Northern Spy and Rhode Island Greening, but they all lagged far behind Macs. Growers planted new orchards mostly with McIntosh. Connecticut Valley Orchard in Westminster, Vermont, began selling apples in 1926, and added 28 acres in 1930 and 1931, bringing its total acreage to 163.

Most of it was McIntosh, sold in New Hampshire, New York, and Vermont.

Despite the industry's growth, New England's export market dried up after World War II. In 1948, John Chandler of the New York–New England Apple Institute (now the New England Apple Association) acknowledged the situation: "For the first time that I can remember, we have had practically no exports this year. The reasons are obvious. Practically no foreign country has the money to buy apples, and our fighting forces, which were supplied with an abundance of fresh fruit, have returned from the war." New England growers have continued to export a modest amount of apples to the United Kingdom, mostly McIntosh to Ireland, but the export market has never recovered.

Until the arrival of controlled atmosphere (CA) storage in New England in the early 1950s, most orchards were a part of diversified farms. "Very few farms could make it on apples alone," says retired grower Robert Lievens of Woodmont Orchards in Londonderry, New Hampshire.

CA storage changed that, allowing growers to store apples reliably year-round. Developed by Dr. Robert Smock of Cornell in the 1940s, CA storage seals apples inside airtight, refrigerated warehouse rooms until they are ready to be packed and sold, often months later. To retard the apple's respiration, the oxygen level in CA rooms is reduced from

21 to 2.5 percent, and the humidity and carbon dioxide are increased, from 0.25 percent to between 2 and 5 percent, depending on the apple variety.

Until CA storage, freshly picked apples that were not sold within a few weeks of harvest were placed exclusively in cold storage warehouses, where the temperature is maintained between 32 and 34 degrees Fahrenheit. Regular cold storage is still in wide use today. It is less expensive than CA storage, and it is effective for the first few months after harvest. Apples in regular cold storage are sold first and are usually gone by January.

CA storage allows apples to remain crisp throughout the year. This gave New England growers incentive to expand production, planting large orchards with a handful of varieties for the wholesale market. Ricker Hill Orchards in Turner, Maine, expanded from 150 acres to 850 acres, including a 125-acre farm in New York, and retired its remaining Jersey dairy cows after building one of the early CA storage rooms in New England in 1957 (Otto Wallingford of Auburn built Maine's first CA storage in 1956). Ricker Hill has since cut back to 350 acres, but it remains one of New England's largest orchards.

Woodmont Orchards in Londonderry, New Hampshire, was another of the early orchards to invest in CA rooms in the early 1960s, eventually allowing it to stop growing other fruits and vegetables and focus exclusively on apples for the wholesale market. This divestment of other crops to specialize in apples and tree fruit was happening at many farms around New England. Brookdale Fruit Farm in Hollis, New Hampshire, sold its herd of dairy cows in the late 1940s. Lyman Orchards in Middletown, Connecticut, sold its Guernseys in 1962. Allenholm Farm in South Hero, Vermont, kept registered Guernseys and Holsteins until 1965. Dame Farm and Orchards in Johnston, Rhode Island, sold its dairy herd in the 1960s.

In Rhode Island, the emphasis has been on retail sales and farm stands since World War II. The largest grower in the state with about 25 acres is Steere Orchard, a fourth-generation farm in Greenville, Rhode Island, that also once had dairy cows. Most of the state's orchards are now small, with one or two acres of apples and a farm stand or retail store, all that remains of once larger properties that have long since been parceled off to developers. "Housing developments continue to take over prime orchard sites," Rhode Island's Everett Percy Christopher wrote in 1970, "and any appreciable increase of pomological crop production seems unlikely."

Weather events have played a major role in shaping both individual apple crops and the long-term look of the New England apple industry. The winter of 1903/04 was so severe that Rhode Island's

Narragansett Bay froze over, killing many apple trees. A deep freeze during the winter of 1917/18 damaged trees from Connecticut to Maine. Some orchards were unable or unwilling to replant, and the land was abandoned or sold for housing.

A severe winter in 1933/34 devastated New England's Baldwin tree population, as well as many Gravensteins and several other varieties. More than 300,000 Baldwin trees died in Maine alone. Baldwin had somehow managed to come back strong following major losses to cold in 1833–1834 and again in the 1850s. By the 1930s, though, the market had changed, and with hardier varieties, such as Cortland and McIntosh, on the ascendancy, growers were no longer willing to risk their futures on Baldwins. "Hundreds of orchardists found themselves out of business," wrote author Clarence A. Day of the winter of 1933/34, "and the work and care of a lifetime destroyed."

The Great New England Hurricane of 1938 knocked four million bushels of apples off the trees and uprooted whole orchards. The historic storm hit Connecticut on September 21, the twelfth birthday of John "Jack" Lyman Jr. in the middle of McIntosh harvest. "More than 1,700 trees were blown out of the ground, and the crop was decimated," he says. Lyman Orchards played a role in the region's recovery, helping to administer a government procurement program, but

it took years for the devastated areas to rebuild. Growers needed up to five years to return to normal production on trees surviving Hurricane Bob in 1991, while thousands of dead trees had to be removed and the orchards replanted.

Although a bitter cold snap or major storm can engulf the entire region, New England's apple crop has also been damaged by weather events that did not impact the larger population. In 1998, most of the region was blanketed with wet, cloudy weather during the two-week period in the beginning of May when apple blossoms were in bloom. Honeybees and other pollinators could not get out to the orchard in sufficient numbers with the rainy, overcast skies, and New England lost more than half of its apple crop because fruit never formed from the unfertilized flowers. A number of small orchards operating on small margins went under.

Virtually every year apple growers somewhere in New England are hit with disaster. Sunrise Orchards in Cornwall, Vermont, lost its entire 2009 crop to hail, and nearly half of its crop in 2010 due to damage from a late frost. A hailstorm in the late 1960s drove Lyman Orchards into the pick-your-own business. "The crop was devastated, and we could not sell it wholesale," says Jack Lyman Jr., "so we opened the orchard to the general public, allowing them to come in and pick half-bushel paper bags for seventy-five cents."

A severe ice storm in Maine in the winter of 2009/10 killed or damaged thousands of apple trees. Historically early blooms in 2010 and again in 2012 following freak heat waves produced apple blossoms two to three weeks ahead of schedule across New England. In many places, the vulnerable blossoms were frozen and killed weeks later, and a spring storm in 2010 left 6 inches of snow in northern Vermont, resulting in major losses at such orchards as Sunrise.

In 2011 Tropical Storms Irene and Lee dropped more than 20 inches of rain in western New England over a two-week period in late August and early September, taking 10 to 15 percent of Connecticut's apples off the trees and leaving the ground so saturated in western Massachusetts and Vermont that many trees toppled over. For weeks it was difficult to get tractors and wagons into the orchards, and pick-your-own orchards lost customers to rainy weekends.

In addition to meteorological events, New England apple growers have had to weather two food safety concerns in recent years, around the use of the chemical Alar in 1989, and a case of apple juice contamination with far-reaching ramifications in the Pacific Northwest, in 1996.

The Alar scare began with a story on the CBS television program *60 Minutes*. Based on a report by the National Resources Defense Council (NRDC), the story identified Alar as a cancer risk, particularly among children. In the following weeks, actress Meryl Streep denounced Alar on numerous television shows and testified before Congress, demanding that it be banned.

Alar was the brand name for a synthetic growth regulator, daminozide, which was introduced in 1968 and applied to crops, such as apples, to extend their life on the tree. This was especially helpful on such varieties as McIntosh, which often drops its fruit before the apples are fully ripe. But when Alar broke down it left a by-product called unsymmetrical dimethyl hydrazine (UDMH), and this was eventually identified as a potential cancer-causing agent.

The effect on the apple industry was swift and steep. In the space of six months, demand—and prices—plummeted, from an average of $15.46 for a 42-pound box of Red Delicious to $8.29. Some growers had to sell off land to recoup their losses, and some went out of business. The Alar scare "was like a guillotine," says Evan Darrow of Green Mountain Orchards in Putney, Vermont. He was forced to close his packinghouse and sell off some prime land to retire a $500,000 debt.

By the time of the crisis, the Environmental Protection Agency (EPA) had already labeled Alar a "probable" carcinogen, and many apple growers in New England had stopped using it (Alar had even been banned in several states, including Massachusetts). Still, the industry was perceived to have dragged its feet, and it took some time for it to recover.

The 1996 juice incident involved *Escherichia coli* (*E. coli*) contamination traced to a single source, the Odwalla Juice Company in Washington State. This isolated event resulted in far-reaching changes nationally in how apples and other crops are harvested and processed. New regulations for commercial cider—specifically the requirement that it be pasteurized—put many of New England's small producers out of business.

The crisis began after one child died and more than 60 people became ill after drinking Odwalla fresh apple juice. Odwalla immediately recalled all its products containing apple or carrot juice, and in 1998 pleaded guilty to 16 misdemeanor charges of selling adulterated food products and paid a $1.5 million fine. Odwalla also made improvements to its production line in an effort to avoid future outbreaks, and began to flash pasteurize its juices.

Despite the rareness of the incident and specific remedies for the offending company to prevent its recurrence, the federal Food and Drug Administration (FDA) soon required that all fresh cider be pasteurized, with the exception of small producers who sell at their orchard or farm stand (they must attach a warning label). Some people maintain that pasteurization compromises fresh cider's taste and texture. Many small orchards chose not to invest in the expensive equipment needed to pasteurize and simply stopped pressing cider.

The Odwalla incident also led to new safety measures affecting all of produce, not just apples or juice products. The FDA published *Guide to Minimize Microbial Food Safety Hazards for Fresh Fruits and Vegetables* in 1998, with recommendations for handling water, manure and municipal bio-solids, worker health and hygiene, sanitary facilities, field sanitation, packing facility sanitation, and transportation. While few would argue with the goals of these safety measures, many of the new requirements have been ineffective or redundant, and they are costly for growers to implement.

The New England apple industry shrank by nearly one-third from 1992 to 2012, from 20,150 acres to 14,200 acres. Besides catastrophic weather and food safety scares, New England's apple industry had to contend with other pressures. Its medium-size to small orchards could not match the economies of scale enjoyed by larger orchards in the vast, apple-growing regions of Washington, New York, and Michigan. Instead, many of New England's orchards became more valuable for development than for agriculture, especially in suburban settings.

BATTLING BUGS AND BACTERIA WITH BIOLOGY

Ronald J. Prokopy (1936–2004) of Conway, Massachusetts, was an innovative scientist and influential promoter of a new approach to pest control known as integrated pest management (IPM), a series of low-impact measures for growing apples that has been evolving since the late 1960s, and is now practiced by virtually every farmer in New England.

The goal of IPM is to limit the use of herbicides and pesticides by using natural controls and other low-impact measures to create and sustain a healthy orchard ecosystem. Up-to-the-minute temperature, humidity, and rainfall from the orchard are evaluated by a regional database to help predict the occurrence of disease and develop a response. Growers add nutrients to the soil to strengthen the trees' natural defenses, mow to keep down competition from grasses and weeds, and remove dead, pruned, or infected wood.

Chemicals are only used when a pest reaches a threshold for economic loss, and spraying is limited to an infected block of trees rather than the entire orchard. The trend toward smaller, more densely planted trees makes it easier to target pests.

A main component of IPM is a series of biological controls, such as pheromone traps and the introduction of beneficial insects. Prokopy, a professor of entomology at the University of Massachusetts in Amherst, studied the behavior of the apple maggot, a parasite that bores into fruit and destroys it. As a way to attract and capture the fly, he helped develop the so-called sticky sphere trap. Bright red and about the size of a softball, the sphere resembles a large apple. Once a bug touches its sticky, baited surface, it is trapped. The highly effective spheres are now common sights around New England orchards.

Prokopy studied the maggot fly's life cycle and developed new techniques to monitor its population. Through this and similar research on the blueberry maggot fly and plum curculio, a beetle, Prokopy gave growers more options for treating orchard pests than pesticides.

A native of Danbury, Connecticut, Prokopy earned his doctorate in entomology at Cornell University in 1964. He began at the University of Massachusetts as an associate professor in 1975, and later became full professor. He had a small orchard at his home in Conway in which he grew disease-resistant varieties Liberty and Freedom, among others.

IPM is practiced differently at every orchard, according to its particular circumstances, and it continues to evolve as scientists search for better ways to treat familiar pests and combat new ones.

**A Spencer apple tree, The Big Apple,
Wrentham, Massachusetts**

Averill Farm in Washington Depot (1746, ten generations), Rogers Orchards in Southington (1809, eight generations), Bishop's Orchards in Guilford (1871, six generations), and Blue Hills Orchard in Wallingford (1904, Henry family, six generations).

In Maine, there are McDougal Orchards in Springvale (1779, seven generations), Ricker Hill Orchards in Turner (1803, ten generations), and Randall's Orchard in Standish (1905, four generations). In Massachusetts, there are Dowse Orchards in Sherborn (1778, seven generations), Bolton Orchards (late 1800s, Davis family, five generations), and Meadowbrook Orchards in Sterling (1912, Chandler family, four generations). Rhode Island has Dame Farm and Orchards in Johnston (1890, six generations), and Steere Orchard in Greenville (1930, four generations). In New Hampshire, there are Mack's Apples in Londonderry (1732, ten generations), and Brookdale Fruit Farm in Hollis (1847, Hardy family, seven generations), and in Vermont, Green Mountain Orchards in Putney (1914, Darrow family, four generations).

These are just some of New England's multi-generational orchards. There are plenty of newcomers, too, such as Chuck and Diane Souther, who started Apple Hill Farm in Concord, New Hampshire, in 1978, and Mo and Phyllis Tougas, who purchased a pick-your-own orchard in North-

Despite its losses, though, New England's apple industry has remained resilient and strong. Many of its orchards are still family owned and operated, and have been for generations. In Connecticut, for example, there are Lyman Orchards in Middlefield (founded in 1741, now in its ninth generation),

borough, Massachusetts, in 1981. Tougas Family Farm is already in its second generation, with son Andre in line to eventually take over.

Old or new, New England's apple orchards are experiencing a horticultural revolution that began in the 1970s and continues to this day. The look and feel of an orchard is changing from well-spaced, standard-size trees to smaller, tightly planted trees trained to fruit walls, spindles, or trellises.

For most of New England's history, apple trees have been afforded plenty of space to grow. In 1839 John Jacob Thomas wrote that "where the quantity of ground is limited, and in rare cases, trees may for a time stand within fifteen or twenty feet; but for large and permanent orchards they should not be nearer than thirty feet." For the first half of the 20th century, most commercial orchards planted trees even more widely apart, on 40- by 40-foot grids.

But since the early 1970s, New England growers have been gradually remaking their orchards with dwarf and semidwarf trees. Smaller, more densely planted acreage makes good economic sense for growers by increasing yields, and requiring fewer chemicals and less labor. Dwarf trees are easier to prune and pick. For orchards in urban and suburban settings that lack access to land for expansion, planting more trees on existing land is one way to add to their value. Spacious, graceful orchards of standard-size apple trees, while beautiful to behold, are increasingly seen as an anachronism, a luxury not up to the demands of modern agriculture.

The shift to dwarf and semidwarf trees was made possible due to several new rootstocks developed at the Malling Research Station in England beginning in the 1920s. A rootstock consists of a young (one- to two-year-old) sapling's roots and a slim stem, to which a desired variety is grafted. Rootstocks are developed for such qualities as disease resistance, hardiness, productivity—and size. New dwarf rootstocks have made it possible to plant apples as close as 18 inches apart and to harvest fruit as early as the tree's third year after planting—about half the time it takes standard trees.

The most successful of the new rootstocks is known simply as M-9. M-9 was introduced in the United States in the 1940s, but it languished for more than half a century before it was adopted commercially. Growers initially had doubts about M-9's hardiness, and needed to be convinced that an orchard of dwarf trees could produce as many apples as standard-size ones.

By the mid-1990s, though, M-9's hardiness and productivity were proven, and M-9 and a handful of other dwarf rootstocks came into widespread use. This enabled growers to increase efficiency and accelerate production, and it gave them greater flexibility to experiment with varieties.

The fact that the smaller trees are easier to pick enhances their value, as labor has been a perennial challenge for New England's growers for decades. An unintended consequence of the 20th-century trend toward a few commercial varieties has been a huge change in the way apples are picked. Before refrigeration, growers planted varieties that would extend the harvest as long as possible, beginning at the end of July and continuing to early November. The crop could be picked in a gradual manner using an assortment of local, part-time laborers.

The arrival of CA storage in the 1950s accelerated the trend toward fewer varieties, resulting in a compacted harvest of eight to ten weeks in September and October. The shorter picking season increased demand for pickers while it reduced the supply, eliminating, for example, college students and schoolteachers. The intense, physical nature of apple picking—seven days a week for two months, in all weather except rain—ruled out many others for whom the work was too hard.

Picking apples requires strength, dexterity, and athleticism, especially on the standard-size trees that have dominated New England's orchards for the past three and a half centuries. To harvest standard trees as much as 30 feet tall with huge, spreading canopies, pickers must climb up and down tall, wooden ladders again and again, filling 40-pound canvas bushel bags strapped to their chest, taking care not to injure the tree or bruise the apples. Semidwarf and dwarf trees are between half to one-third as tall as standards, so ladders are smaller and lighter, but in other respects the harvesting process is the same. The canvas bags are emptied into large wooden bins that hold the contents of about 22 bushels, or 850 pounds.

The apple crop cannot wait; ripe apples need to be picked in a timely way or they slowly begin to deteriorate. Since World War II, every year growers have had to scramble to find people to do the arduous, time-sensitive work of picking apples. Most growers today use the federal H-2A Visa program for their seasonal labor. Begun as the H-2 program in 1943, the H-2A program for agriculture was created in 1986. It is expensive, bureaucratic, occasionally unreliable, and constantly politicized in the debate over immigration, but it is the best option available to most growers. Most of New England's migrant apple pickers since the 1980s have come from Jamaica, and before that Puerto Rico and Canada.

For many years New England's apple crop was picked by a variety of domestic workers. In the 1940s and '50s, some of the apples at Lyman Orchards in Connecticut were picked by "Knights of the Road," migrant labor crews that were often unreliable, with plenty of alcohol abuse, says Jack Lyman Jr. Until the late 1980s, Hackett's Orchard in South Hero, Vermont, had local people signing up in advance to pick apples; now there are none.

J. P. Sullivan and Co., in Ayer, Massachusetts, the largest apple-packing facility in New England, hired the wives of GIs at nearby Fort Devens until the reserve military base closed in 1996.

Before H-2A, "we suffered," says Robert Tuttle of Breezelands Orchards in Warren, Massachusetts. "We would hire local crews, but after a morning of hard work in the heat, many would leave for lunch and never come back."

Christiansen Orchard in Slatersville, Rhode Island, hired retired millworkers. "They were not fast," says retired owner George Smith, "but they were steady, and gentle. Then we hired younger kids, and they were not as good. They would work for two hours and then you had to chase them."

Brookdale Fruit Farm in Hollis, New Hampshire, tapped into a number of groups to pick their apples—even prisoners of war. For a long time, Brookdale managed the harvest hiring local residents, family, and friends. During World War II, though, children were excused from school in the fall to pick apples, and German prisoners of war were brought to the farm from Fort Devens. "I remember one prisoner who fixed canvases for us and did a beautiful job," Eleanor Whittemore says. In the 1950s firefighters from Nashua would come to Hollis to pick on their days off.

Brookdale also hired the older children of Canadian parents who had migrated to Nashua to work in its mills. "We would pick them up in an open truck and, standing up in the back, they were driven to the orchard. You could never do that today," says Whittemore. The crew was paid every night, she says, "and the children would ask for change, because paper money went to their parents to help feed their families."

In the 1960s Brookdale tried crews of young people, "but they were not reliable," Whittemore says. "None lasted more than two or three weeks. They did not have the stamina to work long hours seven days a week." The farm then shifted to migrant laborers from Puerto Rico first, then Jamaica.

Mack's Apples in Londonderry, New Hampshire, had a crew of seven African American pickers from southern states return to the orchard for 20 years in the 1950s and 1960s, says Andy Mack Sr., "but the best eventually got full-time jobs in their hometowns." For a time in the late 1970s, Mack's hired a crew of Quakers from New York State. "We loved them. They did a beautiful job. They were perfect but slow, and not very interested in making money. We had them work side by

PRESERVING NEW ENGLAND HEIRLOOMS

Stearns Lothrop Davenport (1885–1973) of Grafton, Massachusetts, did more to preserve heirloom apple varieties than perhaps any other individual in the 20th century. More than 60 varieties grown by Davenport in his 50-acre orchard survive to this day through his efforts. He shipped more than 12,000 scions around the world from the orchard he began in the 1930s.

Davenport's interest in preserving heirloom apples began around 1930, when he was in charge of an American Wood Protection Association project to remove old apple trees and cut them up for firewood. He feared that many valuable apple varieties would be lost, taking their unique qualities, unusual histories, and genetic material with them.

In consultation with researchers at the University of Massachusetts in Amherst, Davenport created a list of 100 varieties worth saving. He spent the rest of his life searching for, grafting, and selling scions from many of those varieties in his central Massachusetts orchard.

His searches took him far and wide. For a small, red, sweet apple named Ramsdell Sweet, Davenport contacted Alice Ramsdell in West Thompson, Connecticut, whose great-grandfather discovered the variety in the 1830s. Davenport learned from her that the original tree was destroyed in a storm in 1926. After considerable searching, he finally tracked down a Ramsdell Sweet scion that had migrated west.

Davenport's search for Washington Royal, or Palmer Greening, a yellow-green apple with mild flavor, took him across the United States and Europe. He finally found a tree just a few miles away in Sterling, Massachusetts, where the variety was discovered in 1855.

According to his daughter, Fayre Nason, Davenport wanted to preserve heirlooms "for study and

side with the Jamaicans, who picked much faster, but after a few years the Quakers got faster, too, so we let the Jamaicans go."

The hippie movement supplied its share of unorthodox apple pickers, too. Douglas Orchards in West Shoreham, Vermont, hired "quite a group of hippies" in the 1970s. "It took them a long time to pick the big trees," says Betty Douglas, "but they had a really good time."

In 2013 the region comprising Connecticut, Maine, Massachusetts, New Hampshire, Rhode Island, and Vermont produced less than 2 percent of the nation's apple crop, which exceeds 200 million boxes. The leading apple growing state was Wash-

show purposes, for possible use in hybridizing to create new and better kinds of apples, to supply scions for those interested, and for future generations to enjoy."

Toward this end, in 1951 Davenport began a partnership with the Worcester County Horticultural Society to maintain his experimental orchard. He continued to buy and sell scions for grafting from across the country, Europe, Canada, and Mexico, until he was 82, when the farm was sold to a commercial grower.

The new owner stopped growing apples five years later, in 1972, but the preservation orchard was preserved, moved to Old Sturbridge Village, the living history museum in central Massachusetts, and jointly maintained with the Worcester County Horticultural Society. More than 60 varieties were planted on an acre of fenced-in land in 1973, including a Davey (rhymes with "savvy") tree from a 1928 seedling that Davenport raised and introduced in 1950.

Davenport died later that year.

When the Worcester County Horticultural Society bought the Tower Hill property in Boylston, Massachusetts, in 1986, Gladys Bozenhard led a group of volunteers grafting scions from the Old Sturbridge Village collection to dwarf rootstocks for a future orchard at Tower Hill. The young trees were raised in a nursery at Tower Hill and planted in their current location in 1990 and 1991.

With input from the Massachusetts Fruit Growers Association and Cornell University's New York State Agricultural Experiment Station, Tower Hill Botanic Garden eventually expanded its collection to 238 trees, two each of 119 pre-20th-century varieties. The Davenport Collection of heirloom apples in the Frank L. Harrington Sr. Orchard lines both sides of Tower Hill's main drive.

ington, which produced about half of the nation's crop on 153,000 acres. New York was second with 42,000 acres, followed by Michigan (39,000), Pennsylvania (21,000), California (11,800), Virginia (11,800), North Carolina (6,800), Ohio (6,300), West Virginia (4,900), and Oregon (4,200). Massachusetts (4,000) was twelfth, behind Wisconsin (4,100). As a region, New England's 14,200 acres of apples would have placed sixth on the national list.

New England's average harvest of fresh apples was above five million bushels, or boxes, annually as recently as the mid-1990s, and in 2013 it was about 3.5 million boxes. Yet New England's apple industry has gradually adapted to its changing circumstances, and a new type of farming has emerged. The region's hilly geography and dense population centers limit the size of its farms, but it has made them more accessible to consumers.

McIntosh continues to dominate in the region, accounting for about two-thirds of the New England crop, and Cortland remains popular, along with Macoun, Empire, and Red Delicious. New varieties, such as Fuji and especially Gala, are becoming more common in the region, among the 30 to 40 varieties that are grown commercially in New England (many more varieties can be found at smaller orchards). The biggest variety to hit the apple industry in the past 50 years is Honeycrisp, an apple developed at the University of Minnesota that had its commercial release in 1991.

Honeycrisp, grown well, is a remarkable apple, large, mostly red, very juicy, sweet with a little tang, and an explosive, light crisp texture. It commands a premium price—nearly double that of some varieties—and is now being planted by growers across the country hoping to cash in on its success. The problem is that it can be challenging to grow, and many Honeycrisp appearing in New England's supermarkets from outside the region are nearly all yellow and lack superior flavor, turning watery or bland. Some growers have stayed away from growing Honeycrisp because of the difficulties it presents. With Honeycrisp, says one grower,

"Everything that can go wrong with an apple will." Most orchards in New England, though, have had success growing Honeycrisp, and in 2014 they are being planted in the region as never before.

Honeycrisp's success instigated a new marketing strategy for new varieties, designed to maintain high quality and prices by controlling the supply. To keep them from being overplanted, new varieties are now trademarked. Both the brand name by which the apple can be marketed, and in some cases the tree itself, can only be used with permission of the trademark holder. This has resulted in the exclusion of New England growers from planting certain new varieties.

Pick-your-own began in New England in earnest in the early 1970s, about the same time that the trend toward smaller trees began, and it has rapidly risen in popularity. Growers keep more revenue by selling directly to consumers, and they save on labor. Pick-your-owns are notoriously messy—as much as 30 percent of the apples can be lost as a result of inexperienced pickers—but they are popular with consumers, and they allow growers to more easily adapt and experiment with small quantities of many varieties, with heirlooms, such as Baldwin and Roxbury Russet, or with newer apples, such as Corail, RubyMac, and Sansa.

While more than half the New England apple crop continues to be grown for wholesale markets, even large farms are diversifying and selling directly to customers, and adding or expanding a retail operation. Green Mountain Orchards in Putney, Vermont, is typical. In the early 1990s it grew apples exclusively for the wholesale market on 275 acres. Now it has scaled back to 125 acres and diversified into blueberries and Christmas trees, with a pick-your-own orchard and a growing retail store and bakery.

The New England apple industry "has almost come full circle," says Robert Lievens of the now-closed Woodmont Orchards in Londonderry, New Hampshire. Almost all the apples from his family's 220-acre orchard were sold wholesale up to

CRAZY FOR CIDER DONUTS

The origin of cider donuts—much to the chagrin of English teachers, the shortened spelling of *doughnut* has become almost universal in New England when paired with *cider*—is unclear, but they are a wildly popular phenomenon in the Northeast, and few New England orchard bakeries survive without them. The question of who makes the best cider donut inspires considerable debate and controversy. These humble, cakelike orbs are nearly as highly in demand as the apples filling the bins or hanging from the trees at many orchards. Why do these apple-infused donuts provoke such fierce devotion, and what is the secret of their success?

No two cider donuts are alike. They are all made with cider and very little shortening and come in two varieties: plain and sugar-coated. The latter are often mixed with cinnamon, as is the batter, giving the donuts their distinctive, lightly spiced flavor. That flavor is equally influenced by other spices, no-

tably nutmeg, added to the batter, but some ingredients can only be guessed at, as orchards guard their recipes like state secrets.

Their texture is what further separates the very good from the truly exalted cider donut. Some are heavier, some a little lighter, but beauty, in this case, is in the taste buds of the consumer. Cider donuts inspire great loyalty: the best ones invariably are those made at one's local orchard. For many, it is love at first bite.

The popularity of cider donuts is staggering. Many orchards have trouble keeping up with demand, especially on fall weekends, and people will endure long lines to satisfy their appetite for this subtly sweet treat. The cider donuts made by Atkins Farms in Amherst, Massachusetts, were one of 12 doughnuts from across the country lauded in 2008 by *Saveur* magazine. On fall weekends Atkins makes upward of 10,000 cider donuts per day.

Lievens's retirement in 2009. But he remembers driving daily as a young man to Old Faneuil Hall in Boston along Route 128 before the interstates were built, in the predawn hours, his small truck loaded with apples. "We would arrive early, park our truck and lock it while Maine potatoes were unloaded. We would go shop for vegetables and grab a cup of coffee, and the sun would just be coming up when we got back to our truck to unload." Those days ended with the arrival of CA storage. "Farms got bigger, and there was more and more wholesale demand.

"But then in the 1980s competing apples arrived from the Southern Hemisphere—such countries as Argentina, Chile, South Africa, and New Zealand—offering good quality and price during late spring and summer, and taking away our CA advantage. At the same time, supermarket chains grew and consolidated, seeking greater volume than many New England orchards could supply."

Orchards had to change their marketing strategy again, in many cases selling off land to retire debts, diversifying their crops, and selling directly to the public. "Everything that was there forty years ago is back," says Lievens.

The diversified farm of the early 21st century, though, requires a new model. Rather than intending to meet the needs of a single family, contemporary New England orchards attempt to lure customers with pick-your-own, elaborate farm stands or retail stores, and bakeries. They have extended their seasons with such fruits as strawberries and blueberries; expanded their product lines with cider donuts, locally made cheeses, honey, and maple syrup; created corn mazes; and offered school tours and wagon rides.

Hard cider is making a comeback in New England, too, having similarly reinvented itself. The hard cider movement now includes commercial manufacturers, such as Samuel Adams's Angry Orchard brand and Harpoon Brewery, both of Boston, and many small, artisanal producers of unique blends bottled and sold like fine wines. The hard cider movement began in the 1980s, when Steve Wood of Poverty Lane Orchards in Lebanon, New Hampshire, replaced his orchard of McIntosh, Cortland, and other traditional, commercial varieties with heirloom apples from Europe—not for eating, but for making his Farnum Hill Ciders. West County Cider, started by the late Terry Maloney of Colrain, Massachusetts, his wife, Judith, and their son, Field, in 1984 became the first winery in the United States to specialize in hard ciders. The couple started Franklin County CiderDays in 1994; held during the first weekend in November, it has grown into a two-day event of tastings and workshops at orchards and restaurants around the county, drawing cider aficionados from around the world.

2

THE FATHERS OF
AMERICAN (WILD) APPLES
John Chapman and Henry David Thoreau

Thoreau picked wild apples off the tree well into fall and winter, when cold nights improved their juiciness and flavor.

They were born within 25 miles of each other in eastern Massachusetts. Their lives overlapped in the first half of the 19th century. Both men were tireless walkers who spent much of their time outdoors. They both championed the American apple, one by planting it, one by his pen.

More accurately, John Chapman ("Johnny Appleseed") and Henry David Thoreau championed the wild apple grown from seed. Neither man cared for grafted varieties. The two never met, and they may not have even known of each other. Chapman planted his apple seeds in primitive orchards; Thoreau was content to let nature sow apple seeds for him. The wild-looking planter of the frontier and the cultured intellectual from New England lived in different worlds. But they had remarkably similar values on several subjects, including apples.

Both Chapman (1774–1845) and Thoreau (1817–1862) are remembered as passionate outdoorsmen, Chapman through his ascetic lifestyle on the frontier, Thoreau most famously in *Walden*, his book-length chronicle about the two-plus years he lived in a cabin on Walden Pond. They shared a belief in the divinity of all things in nature, and they rejected materialism in word and deed.

Both men were closely linked to philosopher, poet, and Transcendentalist Ralph Waldo Emerson (1803–1882), another Massachusetts native. The Boston-born Emerson once described the apple as "the American fruit" and used apples metaphorically in his writing ("We are born believing. A man bears beliefs as a tree bears apples."). Emerson and Thoreau met in 1837 and remained friends for the next quarter-century, until Thoreau's death.

Emerson, like Thoreau, never met Chapman, but they are linked by their religious beliefs. They are two of the most well-known, ardent adherents of the Swedish theologian Emanuel Swedenborg.

While Chapman and Thoreau came to similar conclusions about nature and wild apples, they arrived at them from very different circumstances. Thoreau's forays into the wild, while extravagant compared to most of the readers of his books, were merely a departure from his usual, comfortable existence. For Chapman, the outdoors was his home from the time he headed west from Longmeadow, Massachusetts, in 1797 until his death at age 70.

Thoreau left a thoughtful and at times passionate essay about his experience of apples; despite being personified with the apple, there is no record of Chapman's feelings about the fruit that consumed him for 40 years. But many of the attitudes Thoreau expresses in his essay "Wild Apples" are consistent with what is known about Chapman's life.

Few would dispute that John Chapman did more to spread the apple gene in America than any other individual, planting dozens of orchards across two states, Ohio and Indiana. Yet apples are conspicuously absent from the popular stories about him. In virtually all of the surviving legends about Chapman, apples are a mere prop, a backdrop bestowing legitimacy and wholesomeness to the teller's own values. He has been portrayed as a holy man, nature lover, herbalist, vegetarian, teetotaler, businessman, buffoon, midwest Paul Revere, and many more personas, depending on one's point of view. Most of these are only partially true, if at all.

But we have no record of how John Chapman felt about apples. Nowhere in the surviving stories do we gain insight into what motivated Chapman to devote his adult life to sowing apple seeds, often in primitive conditions. His connection to apples is stated as a mere fact, without embellishment or explanation. All we have are a nickname and a list of business transactions. We can only infer from his name and the length and breadth of his plantings that he was passionate about the fruit.

In "Wild Apples," Thoreau's strongly stated preference for seedling apples over grafted ones, his love of cider, and the beauty he sees in even gnarly apples, all read as if they could have been written by Chapman. There is a great similarity between Thoreau's views about apples and the facts of Chapman's life.

Chapman planted his apple orchards from seed in Ohio and Indiana between 1806 until 1845, when Thoreau was not yet 30. Even in this, the legend begins: Chapman has been reported to have planted orchards in more than 30 states.

Chapman was an indefatigable walker from the time he set out from western Massachusetts as a young man on foot to Pennsylvania. He crisscrossed Ohio and Indiana numerous times along rudimentary footpaths and roads, carrying apple seeds with him from western Pennsylvania cider mills. He occasionally rode a horse or paddled a canoe, but usually he walked, over wild terrain.

Thoreau was a great walker, too, albeit within New England's narrower, more civilized confines. His book *Cape Cod* chronicles Thoreau's three walks along the outer edge of Cape Cod between 1849 and 1855, when the road was rough and the towns lightly settled. Unlike Chapman, Thoreau arrived on the Cape by stagecoach, and returned after his journeys to his comfortable Concord home. But even on the sands of the Cape, Thoreau encountered apples and wrote about the stunted, sprawling trees: "I . . . saw on the Cape many full-grown apple trees not higher than a man's head; one whole orchard, indeed, where all the fruit could have been gathered by a man standing on the ground; but you could hardly creep beneath the trees."

Thoreau went further than most men of his era and background to experience nature by spending two years living in a rustic cabin on Walden Pond, but he was effete by Chapman's standards. Chapman lived most of his adult life outdoors, and he preferred sleeping under the stars to even as rudimentary a shelter as a cabin.

Chapman's love of nature had a strong spiritual dimension. He was a proselytizer of Emanuel Swedenborg (1688–1772), whose interpretation of the Bible held that everything in nature—not just plants and animals, but also inanimate objects, such as rocks and minerals—is spiritually divine. Chapman lived by and preached this message to families that took him in from time to time. The American church started by Swedenborg's followers never grew very large, with fewer than 10,000 members at its peak, but his elaborate cosmology attracted a number of intellectuals, including Emerson. On the frontier, where many were poor, illiterate, and focused on survival, Chapman was an anomaly.

Several stories about Chapman affirm his belief in the sanctity of all life. In one, Chapman regrets killing a rattlesnake with his hoe after it had bitten him. The snake was only doing what was natural for it, Chapman is alleged to have said, and he rued his act for years. In another story, Chapman is stung by a hornet trapped in his clothing, but he refuses to kill it, patiently helping it work its way out.

Apples are absent in these and other stories about Chapman's humility and generosity. He was once given a pair of shoes, only to give them away to someone he judged needed them more than he. He saved lame or old horses from slaughter, nursing them to health and giving them to families that could use them.

Apples are incidental to stories about Chapman's business acumen—or lack thereof. He owned little except the widely scattered parcels of land on which his orchards grew, and he did a poor job of holding on to them. Chapman's ability to anticipate the settlers' westward migration and plant apple orchards to supply new settlements has been described as visionary, and his tremendous energy and work ethic made his extensive plantings possible. But he was a poor bookkeeper, he was undercapitalized, and he was often exploited as an absentee landowner. He could just as easily have been planting melons or pears rather than apples in these stories, or even selling pencils, like the Thoreaus.

Another story portrays Chapman as a national hero during the War of 1812, without a mention of apples. Two months after American general William Hull surrendered to British and Indian forces at Detroit, leaving Ohio's settlers vulnerable to retaliatory violence, Chapman warned settlers of the approach of Indian forces on several occasions, including one night in September 1812.

A religious-tinged version of that night ascribes to Chapman the Biblical-style warning: "The Spirit of the Lord is upon me, and he hath anointed me to blow the trumpet in the wilderness, and sound an alarm in the forest; for, behold, the tribes of the heathen are round about your doors, and a devouring flame followeth after them." Such a stilted, long-winded warning, repeated many times, is unlikely. Other accounts of that night assert that Chapman ran 26 miles through the forest from Mansfield to Mount Vernon, Ohio, warning settlers along the way. It is doubtful that he would have traveled on foot rather than on horseback to deliver such an urgent message, especially at night. The reported distance of 26 miles is not the actual distance between the two towns (it is close to 40 miles), but the length of the modern marathon. Both versions of the story mythologize Chapman as a Paul Revere–like hero of the Ohio frontier.

Other legends about Chapman assign him almost superhuman qualities of resourcefulness and endurance. During his first winter in Pennsylvania in 1797, according to one story, Chapman was stranded in a cabin in a 3-foot snowfall, and he fashioned snowshoes from beech branches to make his way out. During another harsh winter, he was said to have survived on a diet of butternuts. Like the rest of the tales about Chapman, neither story has anything to do with apples.

Many of the contradictions embedded in these depictions of Chapman reflect America's struggles with issues of class. Despite his primitive lifestyle, Chapman's connection to eastern intellectuals was evident in his literacy, his obscure and complicated religion, and his Massachusetts roots. These could easily be ridiculed on the frontier, especially when combined with his wild, unkempt appearance, when his energetic descriptions of heaven and earth left his audiences feeling a little uneasy. The storyteller was stripped of his dignity by being assigned a duncelike mush-pot cap and a grotesque physical appearance, smelly, shoeless, in rags. Any comparisons with Christ were dashed by Chapman's gnarly feet. Christ had his feet bathed by Mary Magdalene and washed the feet of his disciples; who would go near Chapman's ugly toes?

More evidence of class conflict was evident in his nickname, Johnny Apple*seed*, rather than Apple*tree*. Trees grown from seed were considered inferior to those planted from grafts. They were sown as freely by birds and animals as by humans, and most were bitter, sour, and uncouth looking, primarily good only for cider. In Thoreau's world back east, seedling apples were being replaced by grafted imports from Europe, many of them good for fresh eating. Apples from grafts were emblems of progress; seedling apples a way of life that was gradually receding, especially in the wake of the temperance movement of the early 1800s, which targeted hard cider.

Educated, well-to-do easterners looked down on the poor, backward lifestyles prevalent along the western frontier. Chapman, with his eastern upbringing, was caught between the two worlds. While he may have seemed full of strange ideas to the settlers, his appearance would have shocked and repelled the civilized world. To the modern man, Chapman represented a fading, impoverished past, symbolized by his nickname. The wilderness in which he lived was seen as an enemy of progress, as was his antimaterialism.

Part of the problem in sorting out the details of Chapman's life is that there were only scant historical references to him until more than 25 years after his death, when he was profiled in a November 1871 article by William D'Arcy Haley in *Harper's New Monthly Magazine*. There are even conflict-

Chapman looks too soft for life in the wilderness in this 1871 image from *Harper's*.

ing stories about his physical appearance. D'Arcy wrote that Chapman had "keen black eyes that sparkled with a peculiar brightness." Robert Price, in his 1954 biography of Chapman, wrote that he had blue eyes. He was described as "puny" in some accounts, and as tall as 5 feet 9 inches in others.

Price's biography includes conflicting firsthand accounts of Chapman's physical appearance. One man who knew him remembered Chapman as "a spare, light man of medium height, and would weigh about 125 pounds. He had fine, dark hair, which he allowed to grow down to his shoulders and brushed back of his ears. His beard was grayish and clipped with shears, never close. He was always clad very poorly, old slipshod shoes without stockings, the cast-off clothes of some charitable miser."

Another contemporary recalled him as "a small man, wiry and thin in habit. His cheeks were hollow; his face and neck dark and skinny from exposure to the weather. His mouth was small; his nose small and turned up quite so much as apparently to raise his upper lip. His eye was dark and deeply set in his head, but searching and penetrating. His hair was black and straight which he parted in the middle, and permitted to fall about his neck. His hair, withal, was rather thin, fine and glossy. He never wore a full beard, but shaved all clean except a thin roach at the bottom of his throat. His beard was lightly set, sparse, and very black."

A third firsthand account describes Chapman as having "remarkably keen, penetrating grey eyes, almost black."

That people who knew him could not even agree on his looks suggests that even during his lifetime people were more interested in what he stood for than they were in the man. People have been filling in the gaps in Chapman's history with their own biases and philosophies ever since. The surest evidence of this is the absence of stories about Chapman's attitude toward apples.

While Thoreau's early life has been well documented, little is known about Chapman's youth, although that has not stopped numerous cartoonists and authors of children's books from inventing childhoods for him. John Chapman was born in Leominster, Massachusetts, on September 26, 1774, the second child of Nathaniel and Elizabeth Symonds Chapman. His mother died of tuberculosis when John was two; Nathaniel, a soldier in the Continental Army, was away in New York at the time. His wife's parents likely took care of John and his older sister, also named Elizabeth, until Nathaniel retired from the army in 1780. Not long after he was reunited with his children, Nathaniel married Lucy Cooley and they moved to a modest house in Longmeadow, Massachusetts, Cooley's hometown. Nathaniel and Lucy had ten children together, making for a crowded household.

Still, John was 23 before he left home, heading west on foot with his oldest half brother, Nathaniel, in 1797. They stopped when they reached the Allegheny wilderness in western Pennsylvania, and while the thread of Nathaniel's story gets lost here, John spent the next seven years learning survival skills and preparing for his life's work.

Additional entrepreneurs established fruit tree nurseries along the western frontier, but Chapman was the most ambitious and energetic. He would choose an area for an orchard where he anticipated westward expansion would be heading, usually by a river or tributary. The Indians, of course, lived on the land first, so there were

some trails to guide him, and there was evidence of prior gatherings. Choosing sites near water was logical, and there were always a few rough woodsmen who preceded Chapman to even the remotest locations. But whether he was a true visionary or not, no one covered as much ground with as much energy for as long as Chapman.

He would clear about 3 acres and plant the area with apple seeds, fencing the orchard in with brush. He would return from time to time to tend the young trees, and when a small community of settlers had formed, Chapman would sell them saplings for a few cents apiece.

He did this in many locations, and he could have been a rich man. Demand for his saplings was high, as the settlers desired the fruit for their diets and needed the trees as proof of their intention to remain on the land.

But when Chapman died of pneumonia, or "winter plague," at age 70, he left little behind. Many of his land claims had been jumped in his absence during his lifetime, or forfeited for delinquent tax payments. Chapman was a poor bookkeeper, and he was bad at collecting his debts. Despite his reputation as a successful entrepreneur, Chapman seemingly cared little for money.

The enduring image of Chapman wearing a tin mush pot on his head has no basis in fact; "not a single authentic instance of its having been actually seen has been preserved," wrote biographer Price. Another myth claims that Chapman enjoyed a favorite variety of grafted apple, usually identified as Rambo or Grimes Golden. The practice of grafting to replicate desired varieties had been common for centuries before Chapman's time, but consistent with his Swedenborgian worldview, he believed that grafting was tampering with nature.

There were practical reasons to carry seeds rather than scions, too. Seeds were more plentiful, easier to carry, and required less care, especially over the distances Chapman traveled in unpredictable conditions over rough terrain. Grafted varieties were not essential to settlers interested in an inexpensive source of sweetness and drink.

Massachusetts native Rufus Putnam, a general during the Revolutionary War, and his cousin Israel had successfully transplanted Roxbury Russets and several other grafted varieties a few miles north of Marietta, Ohio, in 1796. But grafted trees from New England or the Old World remained at greater risk for failure in the uncharted frontier, where little was known about the climate, soil, and other growing conditions. Chapman could not risk making relatively few grafts and having them fail, trusting instead in the random process of natural selection. His countless seedlings accelerated the apple's adaptation to this new country, as only the best and hardiest trees survived.

Unlike Chapman, Thoreau was part of a small, stable family living in a comfortable home in Concord. One of four children, Thoreau studied at Harvard as his grandfather had, and he began a career as a schoolteacher, like his two older siblings. His father manufactured pencils, and Henry David soon gave up teaching to work in the family business, which he did for the rest of his life to supplement his writing income. He was also a land surveyor.

Compared to Chapman, Thoreau was a model of gentility and stability. Yet despite their disparate backgrounds, Thoreau frequently gives voice in his writings to values practiced by Chapman, especially about apples.

The intellectual movement linking Emerson to Chapman and Thoreau was Transcendentalism. Emerson and Thoreau were two of the movement's highest-profile members; Chapman would have identified with Swedenborg rather than the Transcendentalists. But central to all three men was the belief that divinity is revealed in all things in nature.

Thoreau, like Chapman, was alternately gregarious and a loner. Thoreau hovered around the fringes of his community as Chapman lived on the edge of the frontier, desiring society at times but ultimately more comfortable by himself. Neither man married.

Thoreau lived a relatively modest life and preached against materialism; the older Chapman lived his life as if he had taken vows of poverty. Thoreau considered material possessions to be an obstacle to spiritual growth. In *Walden*, published in 1854, nearly ten years after Chapman's death, Thoreau wrote, "I see young men, my townsmen, whose misfortune it is to have inherited farms, houses, barns, cattle, and farming tools; for these are more easily acquired than got rid of. Better if they had been born in the open pasture and suckled by a wolf, that they might have seen with clearer eyes what field they were called to labor in."

Later in *Walden* he wrote, "Most of the luxuries, and many of the so called comforts of life, are not only not indispensable, but positive hinderances [*sic*] to the elevation of mankind," and "my greatest skill has been to want but little," and "a man is rich in proportion to the number of things which he can afford to let alone."

Those are fair descriptions of how Chapman lived his life. He owned little, wore rags, did not care about money, and often gave things away.

But it was in his essay "Wild Apples," published in *The Atlantic Monthly* in November 1862, six months after Thoreau's death, that he rhapsodized about the kind of seed trees Chapman spent his adult life planting and tending. Thoreau examined the apple from anthropological, historic, and spiritual perspectives, eloquently praising the wild tree. "So much for the more civilized apple trees,"

he wrote. "I love better to go through the old orchards of ungrafted apple trees, at whatever season of the year . . ."

The apple was uniquely democratic, almost patriotic seen through Thoreau's eyes: "Most fruits which we prize and use depend entirely on our care. Corn and grain, potatoes, peaches, melons, and so on, depend altogether on our planting; but the apple emulates man's independence and enterprise. It is not simply carried but, like him to some extent, it has migrated to this New World and is even, here and there, making its way amid the aboriginal trees, just as the ox and dog and horse sometimes run wild and maintain themselves. Even the sourest and crabbedest apple growing in the most unfavorable position suggest such thoughts as these, it is so noble a fruit."

This passage recognizes Chapman's methods and suggests his attitude, although Thoreau refers to seedlings that have sprouted without human intervention. Thoreau goes on to defend the wild apple's flavor, relishing its tartness and patiently waiting for it to mellow over time. The wild apples he encountered in the New England countryside "are more memorable to my taste than the grafted kinds; more racy and wild American flavors do they possess, when October and November, when December and January, and perhaps February and March even, have assuaged them somewhat. An old farmer in my neighborhood, who always selects the right words, says that 'they have a kind of bow-arrow tang.'"

Given the range of passions suggested by Chapman's lifestyle and his love of nature, it seems likely that when it came to the apple, he was more of a romantic than a pragmatist. Thoreau was, too, rejecting the view that wild apples are homely and outdated, offering a loving portrait instead, in a manner that evokes Chapman's deeds, if not his words. "Almost all wild apples are handsome," Thoreau writes. "They cannot be too gnarly and crabbed and rusty to look at. The gnarliest will have some redeeming traits even to the eye. You will discover some evening redness dashed or sprinkled on some protuberance or in some cavity. It is rare that the summer lets an apple go without streaking or spotting in on some part of its sphere. It will have red stains, commemorating the morning and evenings it has witnessed; some dark and rusty blotches, in memory of the clouds and foggy, mildewy days that have passed over it; and a spacious field of green reflecting the general face of Nature—green even as the fields, or a yellow ground, which implies a milder flavor—yellow as the harvest or russet as the hills."

Similarly, Thoreau's take on cider, while more primitive even than the juices pressed by the purchasers of Chapman's trees on the frontier, reveals a reverence and awe worthy of the older man. "Before the end of December, generally, (the apples) experience their first thawing. Those which a month ago were sour, crabbed, and quite unpalatable to the civilized taste, such at least as were frozen while sound, let a warmer sun come to thaw them, for they are extremely sensitive to its rays, are found to be filled with a rich, sweet cider, better than any bottled cider that I know of and with which I am better acquainted than with wine. All apples are good in this state, and your jaws the cider press."

By the end of his essay, though, Thoreau acknowledges the passing of the apples personified by Chapman. "The era of the wild apple will soon be past," he concludes. "It is a fruit which will probably become extinct in New England. You may still wander through old orchards of native fruit of great extent, which for the most part went to the cider mill, now all gone to decay. . . . Since the temperance reform and the general introduction to grafted fruit, no native apple trees, such as I see everywhere in deserted pastures and where the woods have grown up around them, are set out. . . .

"I doubt if so extensive orchards are set out today in my town as there were a century ago, when those vast, straggling cider-orchards were planted, when men both ate and drank apples, when the pomace heap was the only nursery, and trees cost nothing but the trouble of setting them out."

3

THE ORCHARD

OF THE

Early 21st Century

**Blue Hills Orchard,
Wallingford Center, Connecticut**

Some things about the orchard are eternal. Three main phases or events that occur every spring and early summer go a long way in determining the fall apple crop:

1. Spring bloom, when pollination occurs;
2. The period when the newly formed apples are at risk from frost damage; and
3. "June drop," when excess apples naturally fall or are intentionally removed from the trees.

The New England harvest begins in August and continues through most of October.

Between November and July, apple trees are planted and grafted, pruned and trained, observed for the presence of damaging pests, and treated, if necessary.

All of these annual activities and events, of course, are molded and shaped by the caprices of weather.

While some aspects of the growing season are predictable and consistent, the look and feel of the orchard is in constant flux, as growers continually seek ways to grow more and better fruit on their arable land. The early 21st century reflects major changes since the 1970s in varieties, the size and number of trees per acre; the methods growers use to deal with pests; and how the apples are picked, stored, and sold.

**Nearly ripe Golden Delicious, Norton Bros. Fruit Farm,
Cheshire, Connecticut**

Planting and Grafting

Apple trees are propagated in two ways: sexually, from seeds fertilized by two parents, and vegetatively, by grafting scion wood, or cuttings, from existing trees onto a rootstock.

The centuries-old practice of grafting is necessary to replicate desired varieties, as seed-grown trees rarely resemble their parent tree. Not all orchards do their own grafting, and not all orchards graft every year. Trees purchased from nurseries have already been grafted with the named variety. But some growers are able to replant orchard blocks without having to remove existing trees by "top-grafting" scions from new varieties on the existing trees.

Grafting typically takes place in the orchard in late winter or early spring. Growers insert the scion into a cut made in the bark of the rootstock about 1 foot above ground, sealing it with a putty-like wax. The rootstock's stem is cut off above the graft the following spring, and a new tree grows from the grafted bud. The tree will now produce the same variety of apple as the one from which the scion was taken, year after year.

In nature, apples are reproduced sexually by seed. The seeds contain genetic material from both their male and female parents, resulting in random combinations of traits that rarely replicate the mother tree. A seed from a McIntosh tree will not grow into a McIntosh, because half the seed's genes come from pollen from another tree. The other tree can be any variety within a mile or two of the McIntosh or the honeybee's range. Many of the progeny will look similar, but each tree's apples have unique characteristics, including flavor, texture, color, and shape. Occasionally in nature, sexually reproduced trees are discovered that have outstanding characteristics. Once identified and named, these varieties are propagated by grafting.

New varieties are also developed artificially in the controlled setting of an apple-breeding program. But it takes thousands of trials and many years for a promising new apple to emerge. David Bedford, director of the apple-breeding program at the University of Minnesota, estimates that it takes about 20,000 seeds to produce a single new variety with commercial potential.

In breeding programs, apple blossoms are harvested when they are still closed, when there is no possibility of contamination from bees or other pollinators. The petals and stamens are removed from the female seed parent. Pollen from the male parent flower's anthers is removed with a tiny screen or comb, and it is spread on the female ovary. Every seed that sprouts will be a unique combination of its two parents. Only the most promising of these—trees that are hardy, disease resistant, vigorous in growth, or that have promising attributes, such as outstanding flavor—are kept, and even fewer are selected for further trials and eventually assigned numbers. The process of discovering, testing, and finally naming a new apple variety may take 20 or more years before its commercial release. It took 21 years for Empire to be released after its discovery in 1945, for example, and 30 years for Honeycrisp.

Apple varieties have been developed for qualities as diverse as vitamin C content (Braeburn) to branch reduction to reduce the need for pruning. Color is considered a key to an apple's commercial success: the purer the green or the deeper the golden yellow, the better. Breeders are continually seeking ways to make red apples even redder, especially the bicolored McIntosh.

Spring Bloom and Pollination

The orchard in bloom is visually stunning, with row after row of lightly scented rosy pink and white flowers bursting open and covering the trees as thoroughly as a spring snowstorm. The radical transformation of the orchard landscape during bloom rivals New England's fiery autumn foliage.

But for growers, spring bloom's beauty is accompanied by anxiety. As mesmerizing as the massed flowers are, there is critical work to be done—and not by the orchard's human caretakers. This one- to two-week period near the beginning of May is when the apple crop is fertilized—or not—by honeybees and other pollinators. Dry, sunny weather is needed to enable these millions of tiny insects to complete their essential work. If rain and heavy cloud cover persist during this time, the bees cannot get out to pollinate the crop, and the result will mean fewer apples. Most years, losses due to poor pollination are modest and scattered across the region. But in 1998, New England lost more than half its crop following an extended period of rain and overcast skies during the bloom period.

While bloom typically occurs during the first two weeks in May in most of New England, there is some variation within the region, and from year to year. It is not uncommon to have breaks of sun in a Connecticut orchard, while another in Maine is drenched or overcast, or vice versa. In both 2010 and 2012, the apple trees blossomed more than a week ahead of schedule throughout New England following early heat waves, putting the exposed flowers at risk when the weather returned to normal. Apple varieties bloom at different times. The Cortland crop at one orchard may suffer huge losses after a period of rain, while earlier varieties, such as McIntosh, and later ones, such as Fuji, are unaffected. At least two apple varieties are needed to ensure good pollination, as the apple has a genetic defense to keep from becoming inbred. When pollen comes from a closely related variety, the blossom shuts down—its pollen tube ceases to grow, and fertilization cannot occur.

Pollination begins when the "king" blossom, the largest and centermost of the apple's five-blossom cluster, opens. In their relentless search for nectar, bees and other insects fertilize the fruit by spreading pollen from the male stamen of one blossom onto the pistil of another, where it tumbles down a long tube and enters the female ovary.

The Italian honeybees used by modern agriculture display amazing efficiency and endurance, in good weather visiting 50 to 100 flowers apiece during as many as 20 trips to the orchard per day. Flatbed trucks carrying honeybees in boxed hives on pallets arrive stealthily at night at the onset of bloom in New England from as far away as Florida and California. The square, white, wooden hives are unloaded when the bees are at their quietest. About one box is needed per acre to supplement the local population of native bees, wasps, and other insects. The imported honeybees stay for the duration of bloom, and then they are trucked to pollinate some later crop at another farm.

Modern agriculture has placed great demands on the nation's honeybee population to pollinate its fruits and vegetables, and one consequence is that

Spring bloom at Hill Orchards, Johnston, Rhode Island. The centermost king blossom opens first.

honeybee health has been in serious decline since the 1980s. Colony collapse disorder is the most dramatic and well-known of the recent threats to honeybees, but they have had to contend with a series of virulent pathogens and such pests as varroa and tracheal mites over the past 30 years.

Colony collapse disorder was discovered in 2006, as beekeepers in 36 states and parts of Europe, Brazil, and India found hives mysteriously empty, abruptly abandoned except for a single live

Honeycrisp, Norton Bros. Fruit Farm, Cheshire, Connecticut

sively with major crops, such as almonds, diminishes the food supply available to the bees before and after bloom, and it sometimes reduces the sources of water. New England's diverse flora in and around the orchard and the many varieties of apples grown may reduce honeybee stress and help sustain the native bee population. Growers are also experimenting with other pollinators besides the Italian bees, such as native bumble- and blue orchard bees, and orchard bees from Japan. More than 100 species of wild bees visit United States apple orchards. None is as effective as the Italian honeybee.

Frost

Once the blossoms are fertilized, the petals slowly drop off and the fruit begins to grow. But for several more weeks they remain vulnerable to a late, hard frost. Blossoms and buds can withstand temperatures in the upper 20s, but colder temperatures will kill them, diminishing part of or ruining an entire crop. In northern New England, this period when the blossoms and young fruit are at risk is not over until the end of May. In 2010 and 2012, early heat waves caused trees to bloom in April, extending their period of vulnerability to frost to a month or more, resulting in significant losses when temperatures fell to the low 20s during several nights in early May.

queen (and sometimes honey and immature eggs and larvae). Some beekeepers suffered losses of up to 90 percent of their hives. The cause of colony collapse disorder is still under investigation, and there is no known cure. Other health threats are likely to surface, too, as agriculture tries to fertilize more crops with fewer bees, subjecting them to the stress of frequent travel and comingling in storage yards, where diseases can spread more easily. Certain pesticides are also suspected of inadvertently killing honeybees.

Monoculture, the practice of growing a single crop or variety in a given area, and used exten-

Growers try to minimize frost damage in a variety of ways, none of which is completely effective. Smudge pots are placed in the orchard to warm the air beneath the trees. Overhead sprinklers are used to coat the buds in a 32-degree cocoon of ice, protecting them from damage. Helicopters and wind machines keep air circulating and the temperature just high enough so that moisture in the air cannot settle on the flowers long enough to freeze.

As is the case with poor pollination, frost damage is often selective, even within an orchard. Trees in low-lying areas with poor air circulation are more vulnerable, whereas trees in higher, open elevations might go unscathed. But there are some years when growers lose their entire crop due to one unseasonably cold night in May.

Thinning, or June Drop

Seeds begin to develop in a pollinated flower as soon as the blossoms drop off. The ovary starts to grow, protected by a thin layer that eventually becomes the apple's core. An outer layer called the exocarp develops into the eating part of the apple, and the calyx (the blossom's green, outer leaves), pistil, and stamen all form the apple's indented, hairy base.

By June, the trees are covered with a huge surplus of small, grape-size apples, nature's hedge against loss from poor pollination and frost. There are so many young apples, in fact, that many must be removed for the tree to thrive; if all this fruit were allowed to develop, it would result in smaller, undernourished apples, and it would put the branches at risk of breaking from the excessive weight. "June drop" is a naturally occurring process, when trees shed surplus apples so the tree can better sustain the remaining fruit. Growers accelerate this process by hand thinning or applying a chemical treatment, such as carbaryl (brand name Sevin), to further reduce the number of apples left on each tree to encourage healthy, good-size fruit.

Before June drop and artificial thinning, trees begin the growing season with two to four times as many apples as eventually survive. After thinning, standard-size trees are left with about 1,000 apples per tree. At 50 trees per acre, that amounts to 50,000 apples, the equivalent of about 500 boxes of medium-size fruit, or 25 bins. Semidwarf trees are thinned to about 750 apples per tree. Planting semidwarfs twice as close as standards (100 trees per acre) increases the yield to 750 boxes, or 37 bins. Dwarf trees are thinned to only about 130 apples per tree, but at 750 trees per acre, dwarf trees yield 975 boxes, or 48 bins. Many growers in 2014 plant their trees more closely, with 1,000 or more per acre.

Weather Events

The bloom and frost periods are predictable times during the growing season when the size and quality of the apple crop are determined. But every year brings random weather events that can affect one or more orchards. The most devastating of these is hail.

In the space of a few minutes, an entire apple crop can be lost during a summer hailstorm, the soft, delicate fruit nicked or punctured by tiny, speeding ice pellets. Apples with light hail damage are still good for eating by forgiving consumers. If the damage is severe, though, the apple can split or discolor, and it can only be salvaged for juice, if at all—the expense of picking damaged apples can easily exceed the return.

There is little growers can do to protect their apples from hail. In such places as Argentina, where hail is prevalent, some orchards have tried placing netting over the trees to protect them. But this is costly and impractical for New England's commercial orchards. As hailstorms tend to be very localized, some growers reduce the chances of catastrophic loss by operating orchards in multiple locations, sometimes miles apart. Still, it is rare for a season to go by without at least a few New England growers' losing all or part of their crop to hail.

Too much or too little precipitation can impact the crop in other ways, especially fruit size. In some years and in some places, irrigation is used to supplement the season's rain, although apple trees, with their deep and wide root systems, are more tolerant of drought than field crops. Heavy rains from late-season storms can fatten up apples before harvest but leave them weaker in storage. Accompanying high winds can knock fruit off the trees before it is ripe.

Sun spots can appear on an apple's skin following an extended heat wave. While it does not impair the fresh fruit, an apple with sun spots may keep less well in storage.

The Fresh Harvest

The best ways to determine an apple's ripeness are simply by tasting it, by observing the color of its skin, or by checking its seeds (they are dark brown or black when the fruit is ripe). When harvest begins, pickers gently wrap their hands around each apple, placing their fingers on either side of the stem. The apple is rolled upward and given a slight twist to keep from removing the fruit spur inside the cluster of leaves at the base of the apple, which contains the following year's bud.

The New England apple harvest begins in early August at most orchards with such varieties as Ginger Gold, Jersey Mac, and PaulaRed. A few places open even earlier with Russian heirlooms

Young apples on the tree, early summer

Duchess of Oldenburg, Red Astrachan, and Yellow Transparent, but their season is short, and they do not keep well.

A number of varieties are ready for picking in September, including McIntosh, Cortland, Gala, Macoun, and Empire. Weather plays a hand in reddening the crop, as cool nights during harvest trigger an enzyme that increases apple color and intensifies its flavor. This is why growers in the southern and western United States are unable to grow a good McIntosh.

The balance of New England's apple crop is harvested in October, with such late-season apples as Fuji, Golden Delicious, and Mutsu. A few varieties, such as Granny Smith and Idared, can be harvested in early November.

The bulk of the New England crop continues to be grown for wholesale markets, and it is harvested by migrant workers from Jamaica and elsewhere, some of whom have been returning to the same orchards for more than 30 years. But pick-your-own operations have proliferated in New England since the 1970s, and they are now common even at larger orchards that continue to sell most of their fruit wholesale.

Pick-your-owns are popular with customers, giving them a rare experience of the orchard, where they can enjoy nature and see how their fruit is grown. Pick-your-owns are also popular with growers, as they keep more of the revenue by not having to pay people to pick, pack, store, and ship it off the farm. But it is messy, with as much as 30 percent of the apples lost to inexperienced pickers.

Postharvest

Fresh off the tree or at the farm stand, apples have a natural bloom that gives them a grayish cast (it is sometimes mistaken for pesticide residue). This dull coating on freshly harvested apples protects them from shriveling and weight loss. Washing the fruit in the packinghouse removes about half the apple's natural protection. A thin coating of wax applied to the apple at this stage can replace the lost bloom while enhancing its appeal to shoppers. By the time many apples are delivered to grocery stores, they are polished and shiny.

The wax is a harmless, natural, non-petroleum-based coating, usually carnauba, a palm leaf extract, or shellac, an insect resin. One or two drops of wax are applied to each apple; one pound of wax will coat up to 160,000 pieces of fruit. Wax has been applied to some citrus fruits since the 1920s, and some fruits and vegetables were waxed even before this to improve their storage life.

Apples continue to respire after they are picked, and unless kept cold they will begin to overripen and break down. Apples that are not sold fresh are placed into regular, cold, or controlled atmosphere storage, where they eventually are sorted, packed, sold, and shipped until the crop is gone, usually by early summer, a few weeks before the following year's apples are ready for harvest. Apples that are damaged or misshapen are sold for processing or juice at considerably lower prices, about 20 percent or less of the price of a fresh apple.

Pruning and Training

Although apple trees can live and bear fruit for more than 100 years, most commercial orchards keep them for only 20 years to 30 years before replacing them with new varieties. Until the 1960s, most growers planted standard-size apple trees with 40- by 40-foot spacing, or 40 to 50 trees per acre. Those orchards are being replaced with smaller trees and increasingly intensive plantings. The trees are planted along narrow rows, are heavily pruned, and are supported on tall posts or spindles, V-shaped trellises, or fruit walls to maximize yields. In addition to increased production, the smaller trees are easier to care for and harvest.

The "spindle" is the central trunk of the tree, and the only permanent part of the tree besides its roots. The apples are supported by the spindle and a framework made of posts and wire. Tall-spindle systems can support more than 1,000 trees per acre, whereas "super-spindle" orchards can be

Late winter, Rogers Orchards, Southington, Connecticut

planted even more closely, to 1,500 trees or more per acre. Branches on super-spindle trees are kept small, no larger than 3/4 inch in diameter where they attach to the trunk, and the tree's height is pruned to 10 or 12 feet so that trees from one row will not shade others.

Most of the year's pruning occurs during winter, when the trees are dormant. Many growers prune every tree every year, shaping them to admit as much sunlight as possible into fruit-bearing areas; training the branches to a trellis, stake, or other support system; and removing injured or dead limbs to reduce the risk of disease.

Pests and Disease

Chemical use is a fact of modern agriculture, and their use in apple growing is no exception. Overall, the United States apple crop is remarkably clean. Growers have powerful financial, health-related, environmental, and moral incentives to limit their chemical use. Since the 1970s, most growers have employed principles of integrated pest management (IPM) to reduce their reliance on chemicals to treat perennial orchard threats, such as apple scab, codling moth, and fire blight, and to combat new pests, such as the brown marmorated stinkbug.

IPM comprises a series of natural controls and low-impact strategies to ward off pests and maintain a healthy orchard ecosystem. With IPM, growers strengthen the trees by adding nutrients to the soil and eliminating vegetative competition. Biological tools, such as pheromone traps, are used to distract, confuse, or lure harmful insects, and beneficial insects are introduced that prey on harmful pests.

Sophisticated recordkeeping, observation, and weather monitoring help predict the occurrence of disease and aid in determining an appropriate response. Chemicals are used only when the presence of a pest reaches a certain threshold for damage and for economic loss, and they are applied during the most vulnerable time in the pest's life cycle. Spraying is targeted to infected trees rather than the entire orchard, and it is applied when the air is still and there is no rain in the forecast. The trend toward dwarf trees means that less spray is needed, and there is less chance of chemical "drift."

A number of controls are in place to prevent all but trace amounts of pesticide residue from ever reaching consumers. Growers have powerful incentives to limit chemical use. Chemicals are expensive to buy and labor intensive to monitor, apply, and record. In New England, the grower and his family typically live right on the farm. If a grower is careless, it can mean economic ruin and the loss or shortening of life for the family. Healthy fruit is a matter of survival.

Many of the permitted chemicals are applied early in the year, before the apples have even formed. All approved chemicals have EPA-prescribed "preharvest intervals," the time between the application of a chemical and before the treated fruit can be harvested. Rain washes off most pesticide residue before picking, but apples are also dunked in water as they enter the packinghouse, bobbing and floating for 20 feet or more before they are buffed by a series of brushes and dryers and reach the sorting line.

When IPM was a new science in the 1970s, researchers were familiar with the orchard's main pests, and there were accurate models for damage and economic loss. A broad spectrum of organo-phosphate materials was used on apples, and it was relatively easy to determine when and where to apply chemicals or use biological controls against certain mites and insects. But organo-phosphates contain neurotoxins that can be harmful to humans with enough exposure over time. The federal Food Quality Protection Act in 1996 reduced the amount of exposure acceptable over a person's lifetime, and this has resulted in significant changes in pesticide labeling, including lengthening preharvest and reentry intervals. The new regulations limit the amount of certain chemicals per acre by reducing the number of applications. The last of the organo-phosphates, azinphos-methyl (trade name Guthion), was phased out in 2012.

Organic apples are difficult to grow in New England because the region's moist climate creates ideal conditions for certain insects and the fungal disease *Venturia inaequalis*, or apple scab, a major problem in the region. Organic-approved pesticides are a part of the treatment plan for these pests and disease, and some must be applied several times to be effective.

Venturia inaequalis is as ancient as the primeval apple forests in the central Asian republic of Kazakhstan, where the modern cultivated apple, of the genus *Malus*, family Rosaceae, originated. (Other fruits in the Rosaceae family include apricots, cherries, peaches, and plums, and raspberries and strawberries.) Apple scab was first reported in America in 1834, on Newton Pippins in New York and Pennsylvania. A small patch of scab on an otherwise healthy apple, while visually unappealing, can easily be removed and is harmless to eat. But excessive scab in the orchard can ruin the crop, defoliating the trees and causing young fruit to drop, or leading to cracked or malformed apples that are unusable.

Complete elimination of scab is virtually impossible in New England, but the potential for severe infestations can be reduced using one or more treatment methods, depending on orchard size. Cleaning the orchard floor of leaves and debris in late autumn is one strategy for small orchards. Flail mowing in larger orchards decreases pseudothecia, the fruiting body of the fungus. Mild applications of urea, a nitrogen compound synthesized from carbon dioxide and ammonia, reduce pseudothecia as well. Mostly, though, apple scab is controlled with fungicide sprays, applied to the surface of susceptible leaves before infection can begin.

Apple scab is just one threat to apples. Forty or more insects and other pests have been known to invade the orchard, and weeds, rodents, and deer can harm the trees or damage the fruit.

One bacterial disease, fire blight, can cause extensive damage to apple trees if not controlled. Growers try to limit its spread by removing infected wood as soon as symptoms appear in the spring; they use bactericides to protect against infection.

Another common threat is the codling moth. Its larvae overwinter in silk cocoons attached to loose bark and other debris around the base of the tree. The white or pink larvae that hatch in early spring are one of the few caterpillars that bore inside the apple. Before the larvae fall to the ground in search of a site to pupate, they fill the tunnels in the apple's skin with reddish brown, crumbly droppings, called frass.

Some spiders and carabid beetles feed on codling moth larvae, but naturally occurring biological controls have not proven effective enough to date. Where populations are high, insecticide applications are used to bring the numbers down to acceptable levels.

Weeds are another orchard "pest," competing with apple trees for water and nutrients and hosting certain plant viruses. In some cases, growth beneath the trees is controlled by mowing, but depending on the nature and extent of the competition, herbicides are sometimes used, especially for tough, invasive vines, such as bittersweet and poison ivy.

In addition to treating pests and disease, most commercial orchards apply ReTain, a naturally occurring growth regulator; it slows down the apple's ripening process. ReTain is applied three weeks before harvest to keep fruit on the tree until it is ripe, pushing the harvest back seven to 10 days. This has been especially propitious with McIntosh, which has a habit of falling off the tree prematurely.

4

Introduction to
THE VARIETIES

**McIntosh, The Big Apple,
Wrentham, Massachusetts**

The photographs and descriptions of 161 apple varieties grown or sold in New England include each apple's

- **Permanent name** (and **major aliases**)
- **Place of origin**
- **Age** (and the **year of its public release**)
- **Parentage** (where known)
- **Harvest date**
- **Flavor scale**, from tart to sweet

The descriptions add unusual stories or histories, plus detail about apple color, crispness, flavor characteristics, and storage quality.

Apple Names

Like the fruit itself, the names and identities of apples are continually evolving, and throughout history many apples have had multiple aliases.

Many an early New England apple was named for the place it was discovered (Bethel, after a village in Vermont), or for the farmer who grew it (Burr's Winter Sweet). As a variety spread within New England and then to other states, it sometimes was rechristened (Champlain, also known as Haverstraw Pippin, Large Golden Pippin, Nyack, Sour Bough, Summer Pippin, and Tart Bough).

Early variety names often reference the apple's flavor or color. As the vast majority of 17th- and 18th-century apples were russeted or yellow-green with mild, sweet flavor, many early varieties have blandly descriptive words, such as *russet*, *sweet* or *sweeting* and *green* or *greening*, in their titles (Hunt Russet, Green Sweeting).

Some early apple names use generic terms, such as *pippin* (Golden Pippin, White Pippin). It means that the apple was grown from seed rather than from a sport limb or a graft (a sport is a random limb that displays different characteristics from its parent). *Pippin* is also a general term for "apple seed," synonymous with "kernel," which appears in the name of some apples (Ashmead's Kernel).

The words *pearmain* and *reinette* (reh-NET) appear frequently in early apple names, too. They are used loosely to describe types of apples. *Pearmain*, as the name suggests, is used for apples with a pearlike flavor, shape, or texture (Blue Pearmain, Winter Pearmain); and *reinette*, an archaic French word applied to a number of apples, possibly translated as "little queen" but of indeterminate meaning (Reine de Reinette, Zabergäu Reinette).

Generations of American pomologists and agricultural writers from the 19th century on, beginning with William Coxe in 1817, have been trying to formalize apple nomenclature ever since, un-tangling these multiple identities and resolving them into a common name and description. Unfortunately, there are many gaps in these accounts, and the stories of the origins and histories of some varieties is permanently fragmented or lost.

The growth of a national market for fresh-eating apples in the early 1900s increased the need for universally recognized names with broad commercial appeal. But although a few apples were given superlatives (Red and Golden Delicious, Howgate Wonder, Rome Beauty), most continued to have prosaic names until the 1970s, celebrating the apple's parentage (Jonagold), a person (Macoun), or place (Fuji).

More recently, the tradition of identifying an apple by person or place has become a marketing liability. Such outstanding apples as Jonagold and Shizuka have been bypassed commercially by apples with carefully vetted brand names touting specific qualities or themes (Envy, Honeycrisp, Pink Lady), many of these new names having no recognizable connection to apples (Jazz, SnapDragon).

Most of these new apples have split identities, though, and they are still known by both their original and trademarked brand names. Apples often have different names in different countries, too (Akane in the United States, for example, is known as Tokyo Rose and Prime Red in its native Japan, and as Primrouge in France).

New apple varieties are always entering the world, either by the design of an apple-breeding program (Cortland, CrimsonCrisp), or by chance in nature (Baldwin, Ginger Gold). These new and emerging apples include sport varieties developed from shoots on the parent tree. In many cases these new varieties and strains are as much about color (Redcort, Redspy, RubyMac)—the redder the better, according to marketers—or disease resistance (Freedom, Liberty) as they are about flavor.

The original name and most common aliases are presented here.

Origin and Age

Apples are grown all over the world. Many of the varieties first grown in New England, not surprisingly, originated in England (Bramley's Seedling, Ribston Pippin), and arrived with the early settlers. A stream of apples from Russia (Duchess of Oldenburg, Red Astrachan) and central Europe (Ananas Reinette, Reine de Reinette) found its way to New England in the 1800s via Canada or the United Kingdom.

This melting pot of varieties reinvented itself again and again on New England soil, interbreed-

Cox's Orange Pippins

ing with the native crab apples and one another, resulting in some interesting varieties that became popular for a generation or two before fading into memory (Aunt Hannah, Hartford Sweeting). Others endure to this day (Northern Spy, Rhode Island Greening, Roxbury Russet).

Apples have migrated freely from state to state, coast to coast, since the earliest Westward Expansion, and they travel in both directions. New England's orchards still feature apples developed by now-defunct apple-breeding programs in Idaho (Idared) and Ohio (Holly), and chance seedlings from such places as New Jersey (Winesap), West Virginia (Golden Delicious), and Wisconsin (Wolf River).

While nature will always produce new strains just waiting to be discovered and propagated, many new varieties today are the product of apple-breeding programs. The closest of these to New England is Cornell University's New York State Agricultural Experiment Station in Geneva, New York, which has produced nearly 70 varieties over the past century, including Cortland, Empire, Jonagold, and Macoun.

Apple breeding has been reduced to just a few programs in the United States, though. In addition to Cornell's, the most active programs over the past century are at the University of Minnesota (Honeycrisp, Zestar!), and a joint program of

Purdue University in Indiana, Rutgers University in New Jersey, and the University of Illinois (PRI) (Enterprise, Jersey Mac). The only other domestic apple-breeding program, at Washington State University, is the newest. Started in 1994, it has not yet produced any new varieties of note.

Outside the United States, apple-breeding programs in New Zealand and Canada have been the most prolific and influential when it comes to varieties grown in New England (Braeburn and Gala were developed in New Zealand, for example; Spartan and Spencer in Canada). Apple-breeding programs in a number of other countries have produced varieties of worldwide fame that have adapted well to New England's soil and climate. Japan developed Fuji, Mutsu, and Shizuka, for example; Elstar and Karmijn de Sonnaville are from the Netherlands.

The origin and age of many apples can be difficult to discern or authenticate. There are no surviving records of most early apples from Europe and Russia. Age can generally be traced to a range of years or a century, but some of these apples may be much older than records indicate. The same is true for some varieties discovered in New England, albeit on a smaller timescale. Many first references to apples use vague phrases, such as "the original tree has been standing for years," or fail to mention age altogether. Similarly, the place of origin is often imprecise, indicating a county or region rather than a specific town.

A chance seedling (nature's way of producing new varieties) by definition has unknown parents. In some cases, the proximity of other varieties and similar growing habits strongly suggest one or more parents. While probable, these are impossible to prove.

Even within controlled environments, apple-breeding programs can make mistakes, most famously with Honeycrisp, which was incorrectly identified by the University of Minnesota as a cross between Honeygold and Macoun when it was released in 1991. DNA testing refuted this in 2004, and it was eventually determined that Honeycrisp is the offspring of Keepsake and a numbered sapling long since destroyed.

Since the early 1800s, an apple's age is typically presented two ways: the year the seedling was discovered, and the year it was commercially released (this year appears within parentheses). There can be a gap of up to 40 years between the two dates, during which time the apple is evaluated in extensive orchard trials for its horticultural tendencies, disease resistance, consistency of fruit and production, and storage qualities.

It took nearly 70 years from the time John McIntosh discovered the apple that bears his name on his Ontario farm until his son released it in 1870.

Harvest Dates

Even within a small region, such as New England, harvest dates can vary a week or more north to south, depending on climate and location.

- **Early season** refers to apples that generally ripen in the region in late July or August.
- **Midseason** describes apples that typically ripen in September.
- **Late-season** apples are ready for picking from October on.

From 1990 to 2010, harvest dates have been historically early, a possible sign of climate change. Normal harvest time for McIntosh apples has gradually advanced from around September 10 to the end of August in parts of New England. The earlier harvest corresponds to an earlier spring bloom, which has shifted from the last week in May in the 1960s to Mother's Day weekend (about May 10) by 2000 to the beginning of May in 2010.

Flavor

Apple flavor is rarely absolute. There can be subtle differences in the taste of a variety depending on where it was grown and how it was harvested and stored. Flavor is subjective, too, and sometimes a single apple is not representative of the whole.

Each apple is ranked on a "tart-to-sweet" scale when it is freshly picked, based on whether it is

(T) mostly tart; (2) more tart than sweet; (3) balanced between sweet and tart; (4) more sweet than tart; or (S) mostly or all sweet.

The term *tart* is synonymous with "sour" or "acid."

The flavor of many apples changes over time and in storage, often becoming juicier, sweeter, and more intense or complex.

Flesh

Apple flesh is described by its texture first, then by color, and fragrance (where it exists), using these terms:

Dense—Harder to bite into than any other texture. These varieties tend not to bruise easily and they store well, making them ideal for shipping (Fuji, Pink Lady).

Crisp—More yielding than a dense-fleshed apple, but more hard than tender (Empire, Golden Delicious). This description fits the vast majority of apples.

Tender—Still crisp, but with a little less resistance (Cortland, McIntosh).

Light crisp—A distinctively crisp texture, almost airy, but exploding with juice (Honeycrisp, Jonagold).

Storage

How well an apple keeps has been less of an issue for consumers and growers since the advent of refrigeration in the early 1900s, and the development of controlled atmosphere (CA) storage in the 1940s, which brings the apple's respiration to a virtual halt inside sealed rooms. Still, some apple varieties store better than others.

Apples continue to ripen and respire at different rates after they are picked, to different effect. In many instances, an apple develops more complex and pronounced flavor months after it is harvested (Esopus Spitzenburg, Idared, Ribston Pippin, Suncrisp).

All varieties gradually deteriorate if not kept cold or after they have been removed from storage. Some develop harmless spots or a greasy skin, which put off some consumers.

The texture of many apples changes postharvest, gradually softening. But the days of the "mealy Mac" are over, thanks to CA storage and the growth inhibitor 1-methylcyclopropene (better known as 1-MCP or SmartFresh). Kept cold (35° to 40°F), McIntosh are now available throughout most of the year, retaining their tender crunch and tartness.

Juiciness

With few exceptions, all apples are juicy. The only difference is degree, and this varies depending on the variety and season. Some apples, such as Honeycrisp and McIntosh, are exceptionally juicy at the time of harvest. Some, such as Idared, develop their juiciness in storage. Even dry apples, such as Sheep's Nose, though, produce ample juice when pressed.

Color, Size, and Shape

The varieties are organized by color:

- **Multicolored**
- **Red | Pink | Orange**
- **Green | Yellow**
- **Russeted**

Two additional categories group apples according to their availability or usage:

- **Restricted** (managed varieties sold in, but not grown in New England)
- **Cider** (apples grown exclusively or primarily for juice)

Within each section, apples appear alphabetically.

Apple color, like apple flavor, is rarely absolute. No two apples are alike, even from the same variety. Most varieties feature kaleidoscopic splashes of two or more colors varying from apple to apple. The closest to a universally monochromatic apple is Red Delicious; even such varieties as Golden Delicious and the green Granny Smith can appear with an occasional pink blush, and Idareds sometimes have yellow highlights.

Such apples as Honeycrisp appear anywhere from solid red to mostly yellow. Gala's color deepens during the season and in storage, from yellow to orange to red.

Many apples have some russeting, especially around their stems, consistently or in a given year. Russet appears as a rough patch on an otherwise smooth skin, drizzled like a glaze over the apple's top, or in intricate patterns as random as hoarfrost. Some varieties are completely covered in russet.

Lenticels are the small dots or pores on an apple's skin through which it respires.

Bloom is a naturally occurring film that helps an apple retain moisture. It tends to dull the apple's appearance or give it a waxy look and feel, and it is sometimes mistaken for pesticide residue. It is harmless to eat.

Blush is an area of spot color with soft edges. It usually results from exposure to the sun.

Apple size is described as **large**, **medium-size**, or **small**, or a range of these.

Apple shape is **round** (McIntosh), **flat** (Bramley's Seedling), **oblate** (such as Lady—when an apple is both round and flat), **irregular** or **lopsided** (King of Tompkins County, York), **boxy** (Macoun), **ribbed** (Calville Blanc d'Hiver), or **conical** (Red Delicious).

Russeted Apples

Russet is harmless, naturally occurring rough skin that appears on many varieties. It may cover its entire surface or a small portion of each apple, especially around the stem. It can appear as fine, scattered mesh (Orleans Reinette), in patches (Belle de Boskoop), or as a solid coat (Pomme Grise). Its texture is like that of fine to medium sandpaper.

A Roxbury Russet on the tree

Russet can result from a number of factors, including frost and cool or wet weather in late spring. Some varieties are more susceptible to spot russet than others (yellow apples, such as Golden Delicious, tend to have more russet than do red apples), while some, such as Hudson's Golden Gem, are consistently covered with russet over half or more of their skin.

Restricted (Managed or Club) Varieties

To remain profitable, New England's growers continually reinvent themselves to meet the demands of a changing marketplace. Successful apple growers are scientists, horticulturalists, and environmentalists, but they must also be good at running a business.

Apple growing is a way of life, and it is hard work that makes many demands. While many of the region's commercial orchards have failed over the past century, New England growers of all kinds have managed to thrive in an increasingly competitive environment filled with snack foods, other fruits, and new apple varieties from outside the region.

For many years, new apples have been patented, entitling their inventors to 20-year royalties on trees. After that, the tree enters the public domain, and growers can legally graft it.

Increasingly, these new apples are trademarked, not just patented. With the 1989 arrival of Pink Lady—the protected brand name for an Australian apple called Cripps Pink—new varieties began to be trademarked, a permanent designation that allows its holder to control supply, price, and quality by restricting who can grow it. Members of a club, or sometimes a single company, can control exclusive rights to grow and market these apples.

In some cases, mostly with early trademarked varieties, New England growers can still access a new variety by paying a royalty or selling it by its original, rather than trademarked, name. But New England growers are legally enjoined, prevented, from growing certain new varieties.

A number of new apples are appearing in New England supermarkets for the first time for a limited time, on a limited basis. The new apples listed here are just a sampling of what New Englanders can expect from around the world—but not from New England—in the coming years.

Cider Apples

Almost any apple becomes an asset in juice, no matter how tart or bitter it may be whole, regardless of its size, whether it is brand new or an heirloom, or gnarly, russeted, bruised, nicked, or misshapen, from England or Japan. Apples gain new life as juice.

Some varieties are dedicated to making juice, and a sampling of them are presented here. Most are inedible "spitters," but become a pleasure to imbibe when pressed into juice and fermented, either alone or blended with juice from other varieties.

Apple juice is the clear, golden, stable liquid sold in bottles in grocery aisles.

Fresh cider is America's term for the brown, unfiltered apple juice sold at farm stands, farmers' markets, orchards, and in the produce sections of most grocery stores. It keeps for a few weeks.

Hard cider is the lightly alcoholic drink fermented from fresh cider.

In this, as with football (soccer in the United States) and the metric system, America is out of step with the rest of the world. In Europe and elsewhere, *cider* is synonymous with "hard cider." Everything else, to Europeans, is simply apple juice.

Multicolored Apples

Baldwin | Ball, Butters, Steele's Red Winter, Woodpecker)

ORIGIN	DISCOVERED	RELEASED
Wilmington, Massachusetts	1740	
PARENTAGE	**HARVEST**	**FLAVOR SCALE**
unknown	Late season	T 2 **3** 4 S

Baldwin is one of the best New England apples, and one of the oldest. It is large and conical, with crimson red over a coppery green skin. Its cream-white flesh is crisp and juicy. It is aromatic with a spicy, sweet-tart flavor, and it holds its shape when cooked. An outstanding apple for fresh eating, it is also good baked, especially in pies. It stores very well.

Although its parents are a mystery, Baldwin has a well-documented history. It was first named Woodpecker because the tree was popular with those birds. Its cultivation passed from John Ball, owner of the original orchard in Wilmington; to William Butters, who later purchased the land; and finally Colonel Loammi Baldwin, who gave the apple its permanent name.

While Colonel Baldwin (1744–1807) is best known for the apple, he was a man of many accomplishments: a Revolutionary War veteran who crossed the Delaware with Washington and commanded the Woburn Regiment during the Battle of Concord and Lexington; a fellow of the American Academy of Arts and Sciences; an elected member of the Massachusetts General Assembly; high sheriff of Middlesex County; and he is known as the "Father of American Civil Engineering."

His engineering feats include the nine-year construction of the Middlesex Canal beginning in 1794, which connected the Merrimack River to Boston Harbor. While working on the project, Baldwin visited the Butters farm and obtained scion wood from the original Woodpecker tree. From these he planted a row of trees near his home in Woburn and gave scions to friends.

Adding to his legacy as a man of apples, Baldwin was a second cousin to John Chapman ("Johnny Appleseed").

Introduced commercially around 1784, by 1850 Baldwin was the Northeast's most popular apple, more widely grown in the United States than any other variety. It remained so for more than 50 years. Its popularity began to wane in the early 1900s.

Baldwin's availability took a precipitous decline following a devastating freeze during the winter of 1934 that wiped out more than half of its numbers, but in recent years it has been making a modest comeback.

Ben Davis

ORIGIN	DISCOVERED	RELEASED
Kentucky, Tennessee, or Virginia	Early 1800s	
PARENTAGE	**HARVEST**	**FLAVOR SCALE**
unknown	Late season	T 2 3 **4** S

Ben Davis is a roundish, mostly red or red-striped apple over a somewhat tough, yellow skin. Its tender, cream-colored flesh is aromatic, juicy, and has a mild sweet-tart flavor. It stores exceptionally well.

Discovery of Ben Davis is credited to three southern states, none definitively, but it had spread throughout these states and parts of the Midwest well before the Civil War. It is not widely grown in the Northeast, but it is a parent of one of New England's most popular apples, Cortland.

Bramley's Seedling

ORIGIN	DISCOVERED	RELEASED
Southwell, Nottinghamshire, England	Early 1800s	1876
PARENTAGE	**HARVEST**	**FLAVOR SCALE**
unknown	Late season	T **2** 3 4 S

Bramley's Seedling is a round, flat apple, green with strawberry red streaks or patches and prominent lenticels. Its cream-colored flesh is coarse-textured and moderately juicy. It is aromatic, with a nicely balanced sweet-tart flavor with hints of citrus. As with a few other apple va-

rieties, such as Cortland, the skin of Bramley becomes naturally greasy in storage, but it keeps well.

Bramley's Seedling was raised from seed in the cottage garden of Mary Ann Brailsford between 1809 and 1813, and the original tree is still living and bearing fruit. Matthew Bramley brought the property in 1848, and the apple bearing his name was introduced commercially in 1876. It is a favorite among cider makers due to its juiciness and balanced flavor, and it continues to be England's most popular cooking apple.

Brock

ORIGIN		DISCOVERED	RELEASED
Alfred, Maine		1934	1966
PARENTAGE		HARVEST	FLAVOR SCALE
Golden Delicious × McIntosh		Late season	T 2 3 **4** S

Brock is a large, round or boxy, reddish apple with a green or yellow blush. It has crisp, juicy, cream-colored flesh that is mostly sweet, with a little tartness.

Brock was developed in 1934 by Russell Bailey, a longtime plant breeder at the University of Maine, and named for grower Henry Brock of Alfred, Maine, one of the trial growers of the variety. The sole variety developed at the University of Maine Cooperative Extension at Highmoor Farm in Monmouth, Brock has the same parentage as Spencer, yet they are distinctly different apples.

Cameo | Carousel

ORIGIN	DISCOVERED	RELEASED
Washington	1987	1998
PARENTAGE	**HARVEST**	**FLAVOR SCALE**
unknown	Late season	T 2 **3** 4 S

Cameo is slightly conical with a thin, light yellow skin with heavy red striping. Its flesh is crisp and juicy, and it has outstanding sweet-tart flavor.

A chance seedling found by Darrel Caudle near Dryden, Washington, Cameo may be a cross between Red Delicious and Golden Delicious.

Corail | Piñata, Pinova, Sonata

ORIGIN	DISCOVERED	RELEASED
Germany	2000	
PARENTAGE	**HARVEST**	**FLAVOR SCALE**
Golden Delicious × Cox's Orange Pippin × Duchess of Oldenburg	Late season	T **2** 3 4 S

Corail has a conical shape and streaks of bright red over a yellow-orange skin. Its crisp and juicy white flesh resists browning when sliced. Corail's flavor has a tropical tinge, with hints of pineapple or citrus.

Corail is a trademarked variety marketed under the name Piñata, and Stemilt Growers of Wenatchee, Washington, holds exclusive rights to grow, market, and sell it in the United States. Some smaller growers had already purchased Corail or Pinova, and they are allowed to continue to grow and sell the apples using those names.

Multicolored Apples

Cortland

ORIGIN		DISCOVERED	RELEASED
Geneva, New York		1898	1915
PARENTAGE		HARVEST	FLAVOR SCALE
Ben Davis × McIntosh		Midseason	T **2** 3 4 S

The all-purpose Cortland has been a New England staple for the past century. A large apple, Cortland has a deep red skin with green and yellow streaks. It has crisp, white flesh, and a sweet-tart flavor that is similar to but slightly less tangy than that of McIntosh, and it is moderately juicy. It holds its shape well when baked, making it an excellent pie apple. It is so good cooked, in fact, that it is sometimes overlooked as a fresh-eating apple, although it has outstanding crispness and flavor. It is particularly good in salads, as its white flesh browns slowly after slicing.

Cortland owes much of its flavor to its McIntosh parent, with its crisp texture, striping, and size characteristic of its other parent, Ben Davis. Cortland develops a naturally greasy look and feel in storage, another feature of Ben Davis. Cortland ripens a little later than McIntosh, stores better, and often is larger and brighter in color.

It was developed at the New York State Agricultural Experiment Station.

Cox's Orange Pippin

ORIGIN		DISCOVERED	RELEASED
Colnbrook Lawn, Berkshire, England		1825	
PARENTAGE		HARVEST	FLAVOR SCALE
Ribston Pippin × unknown		Midseason	T **2** 3 4 S

Cox's Orange Pippin is a strikingly beautiful apple with flavor to match. It is medium-size, round, and predominantly orange-red with red striping over a yellow base. Its cream-colored flesh is crisp and juicy. It has outstanding flavor—spicy, aromatic, and complex. The website www

.orangepippin.com describes Orange Cox's Pippin as "a variety for the connoisseur, who can delight in the appreciation of the remarkable range of subtle flavors—pear, melon, freshly squeezed Florida orange juice, and mango are all evident in a good example." It is highly valued in cider as well as for fresh eating.

Richard Cox, a retired brewer from London, raised the apple from seeds of a Ribston Pippin. A favorite in its native England since the 19th century, Cox's Orange was introduced in America about 1850. It is making a modest comeback in New England orchards.

Creston

ORIGIN	DISCOVERED	RELEASED
Summerland, British Columbia	1998	
PARENTAGE	**HARVEST**	**FLAVOR SCALE**
Golden Delicious × NJ 381049	Late season	T 2 3 **4** S

Creston is a large, conical apple resembling Jonagold in shape, color, and flavor. Yellow with a red blush or stripes, its yellow flesh is crisp, juicy, and sweet. There are mixed reviews on its storage ability; some say it stores better than Jonagold; others, that it can become greasy or soft in storage.

Creston was developed at Canada's Pacific Agri-Food Research Centre.

Duchess of Oldenburg

ORIGIN	DISCOVERED	RELEASED
Russia	Age unknown	
PARENTAGE	**HARVEST**	**FLAVOR SCALE**
unknown	Early season	T **2** 3 4 S

Duchess of Oldenburg is a stunning apple with beautiful, yellow-and-red-striped skin. Its flesh is yellowish, firm, crisp, and juicy. A highly aromatic apple, it has excellent culinary qualities, but it does not store well.

Multicolored Apples

Duchess of Oldenburg came to America via England, where it arrived from Russia around 1815. It was one of several Russian varieties that made apple growing easier in America's colder regions. Along with Alexander, Tetofsky, and Red Astrachan, Duchess of Oldenburg was imported by the Massachusetts Horticultural Society around 1835.

In European nurseries, Oldenburg was propagated under the names Charlamowsky and Borowitsky. An extremely hardy variety, Oldenburgs "kept up the hope of prairie orchardists in times of great discouragement," according to S. A. Beach's *The Apples of New York, volume 2.*

Early McIntosh

ORIGIN		DISCOVERED	RELEASED
Geneva, New York		1909	1923
PARENTAGE		HARVEST	FLAVOR SCALE
Yellow Transparent × McIntosh		Early season	T **2** 3 4 S

Early McIntosh is largely red with highlights of yellow or green, and prominent white lenticels. Its tender white flesh is juicy, and it has sweet flavor with hints of strawberry. It is good for fresh eating, but like many early-season apples it does not store well. Early McIntosh was developed at the New York State Agricultural Experiment Station.

Elstar

ORIGIN	DISCOVERED	RELEASED
Netherlands	1950s	1972
PARENTAGE	**HARVEST**	**FLAVOR SCALE**
Golden Delicious × Ingrid Marie	Late season	T **2** 3 4 S

Elstar is a medium-size to large yellow apple with red streaking, and its cream-colored flesh is crisp, with sweet-tart flavor. It is a good fresh-eating and culinary apple, and has been likened to Jonagold. As it matures, its flavor mellows.

A cross between Golden Delicious and Ingrid Marie, a variety from Denmark dating back to 1910, Elstar was first grown in the Netherlands. It was distributed to America in the 1970s. Although it favors a cooler climate, it is not widely grown in New England.

Empire

ORIGIN	DISCOVERED	RELEASED
Geneva, New York	1945	1966
PARENTAGE	**HARVEST**	**FLAVOR SCALE**
McIntosh × Red Delicious	Midseason	T 2 3 **4** S

Empire is a medium-size, round apple with a deep red skin and yellow and green highlights. A cross between McIntosh and Red Delicious, it has some tartness but is sweeter than McIntosh. Empires have crisp, juicy, white flesh that does not bruise easily. It is outstanding for fresh eating and good for all culinary uses.

Empire is a relatively new variety, raised by Roger D. Way at the New York State Agricultural Experiment Station.

Multicolored Apples

Fortune

ORIGIN		DISCOVERED	RELEASED
Geneva, New York		1995	
PARENTAGE		**HARVEST**	**FLAVOR SCALE**
Empire × Schoharie Spy		Late season	T **2** 3 4 S

Fortune is a large, red apple with green striping; its crisp, cream-colored flesh, both sweet-tart and spicy, has a sprightly flavor. It is outstanding for fresh eating, in pies, and in sauce, and it keeps well in storage.

A cross between Empire and Schoharie Spy, a red sport of Northern Spy, Fortune was developed at the New York State Agricultural Experiment Station.

Fuji

ORIGIN		DISCOVERED	RELEASED
Japan		1939	1962
PARENTAGE		**HARVEST**	**FLAVOR SCALE**
Red Delicious × Ralls Janet		Late season	T **2** 3 4 S

Fuji is a medium-size to large, yellow-green apple covered by a heavy pink blush. It has dense, white, juicy flesh, with a sweet flavor owing primarily to its Red Delicious parent. Fuji's other parent, the Virginia heirloom Ralls Janet, is a good eating apple known for its late bloom, making Fuji less susceptible to frost damage. Fuji is a great keeper, maintaining its quality for several weeks left in a fruit bowl or for up to one year refrigerated.

Fuji was developed in Japan in 1939, and was named in 1962, after Japan's tallest and most sacred mountain.

Gala

ORIGIN	DISCOVERED	RELEASED
New Zealand	1934	
PARENTAGE	**HARVEST**	**FLAVOR SCALE**
Cox's Orange Pippin, Kidd's Orange Red, Red Delicious, Golden Delicious	Midseason	T 2 3 4 **S**

Gala is a medium-size to large, conical, red-orange apple with yellow highlights. Its cream-colored flesh is crisp and juicy. It has a sweet, pearlike flavor, and it is outstanding for all uses, especially for fresh eating. It tends to have a yellowish color early in the season and becomes a darker red-orange as the harvest progresses and in storage.

Gala is now one of the most widely grown apples in the world.

Granite Beauty | Aunt Dorcas, Clothesyard, Dorcas, Grandmother

ORIGIN	DISCOVERED	RELEASED
Weare, New Hampshire	Early 1800s	
PARENTAGE	**HARVEST**	**FLAVOR SCALE**
unknown	Late season	T **2** 3 4 S

Granite Beauty is a large, beautiful apple, roundish, ribbed, with red patches and stripes over a yellow skin. Its cream-colored flesh is crisp and juicy, and it has a rich, sweet-tart flavor with hints of coriander or cardamom.

Zephaniah Breed, who discovered Granite Beauty, wrote in the late 1850s that "no orchard is considered complete here unless it contains a good share of these trees. A good fruit grower here says he would sooner do without the Baldwin than the Granite Beauty."

Breed published this account of Granite Beauty in the *New Hampshire Journal of Agriculture*, which he edited:

"Years ago, soon after the first settlers located upon the farm we now occupy, they paid a visit to their friends in Kittery (now Elliott), Maine, on horseback, that being the only means of conveyance then in vogue. When about to return home, Dorcas (for this was her maiden name—she was now Dorcas Dow, formerly Neull) needing a riding whip, she was supplied by pulling from the earth, by the side of the road, a little apple tree. With this she hurried her patient and sure-footed horse toward her wild-woods home in Weare, then Halestown.

"An orchard being in 'order' about that time, the little tree was carefully set and tended, and when it produced its first fruit it was found to be excellent, and Dorcas claimed it as her tree. When nephews and nieces grew up around her, the apple was called the Aunt Dorcas apple, from the claim she had upon it." As she grew older and her grandchildren grew up, the apple took the name of Grandmother. In another part of the town it was called the Clothesyard apple.

Gravenstein

ORIGIN	DISCOVERED	RELEASED
Germany or Italy	1600s	
PARENTAGE	**HARVEST**	**FLAVOR SCALE**
unknown	Early season	T **2** 3 4 S

Gravenstein is a medium-size apple, slightly blunt and conical, with blurry red streaks on a thin green skin. Its cream-colored flesh is crisp and juicy, with sweet-tart flavor. It is especially good in pies, sauces, and ciders. Gravenstein stores better than most early-season varieties.

An old apple dating to at least the 1600s, Gravenstein was popular in New England from the late 1800s until the 1930s. Its origins are unclear. It probably came from Germany or Italy. It first appeared in Denmark about 1669 and England in 1819. Gravenstein (German for the southern Denmark town of Gråsten) is strongly identified with Denmark—it was declared Denmark's national apple in 2005. It may be one of several European apples imported to the United States by the Massachusetts Horticultural Society in the 1800s.

Hidden Rose | Airlie Redflesh, Red Flesh, Schwartz

ORIGIN	DISCOVERED	RELEASED
Airlie, Oregon	1960s	2001
PARENTAGE	**HARVEST**	**FLAVOR SCALE**
unknown	Late season	T **2** 3 4 S

Hidden Rose is a small, conical apple with light yellow skin with pink blush. Its dense pink flesh is slow to brown, making it a good choice in salads. This sweetly aromatic apple has a pleasing tartness with hints of citrus, but it is not very juicy. It is mainly a fresh-eating apple, though it is used in cooking, especially nice to color an applesauce.

Hidden Rose was discovered as a chance seedling on land owned by Lucky and Audrey Newell near Airlie, Oregon. Although they sent samples to Oregon State University, the variety remained unknown even after the Newells sold the property. In the 1980s, Louis Kimzey, the retired manager of a neighboring farm, rediscovered the tree, and it was soon given the name Airlie's Redflesh (eventually shortened to Red Flesh). In the 1990s, several nurseries grew the variety locally under the name Schwartz. Kimzey and his former employer, Thomas Paine Farms, finally decided to commercialize the apple, and in 2001 they trademarked the name Hidden Rose.

Multicolored Apples

Holstein

ORIGIN	DISCOVERED	RELEASED
Germany	1918	
PARENTAGE	**HARVEST**	**FLAVOR SCALE**
Cox's Orange Pippin × unknown	Midseason	T 2 **3** 4 S

Holstein is a medium-size, round yellow apple with red streaks. Its sweet, juicy, cream-colored flesh is coarse-textured, moderately crisp, and juicy. Its flavor is nicely balanced between sweet and tart, making it a good choice for pie making. It is a good storing apple.

Holstein was discovered by a teacher named Vahldik in Eutin, Holstein.

Honeycrisp

ORIGIN	DISCOVERED	RELEASED
Minnesota	1961	1991
PARENTAGE	**HARVEST**	**FLAVOR SCALE**
Keepsake × unknown	Midseason	T 2 3 **4** S

Honeycrisp has generated more excitement and controversy than any other variety introduced in the United States in the past 50 years. A large apple, it is highly variable in color, from nearly solid red to mostly yellow with red streaks. Honeycrisp features a unique texture that combines plenty of juice with explosive crispness, offering just enough resistance. Its flavor is sweet, honeylike with a hint of tartness. A good Honeycrisp is an exceptional apple. If you bite into one and do not understand what all the fuss is about, try another.

Honeycrisp does not store well, though, and it is notoriously difficult to grow. Even in New England, where it grows well, some growers have declined to plant it because they are not convinced they can produce Honeycrisp of superior quality.

If poorly grown or stored improperly, its unique flavor can become bland and watery. Yet demand for good Honeycrisp is so high, growers across the country are planting them indiscriminately, leading to concerns that fruit quality and the rate of return to growers eventually will suffer—good Honeycrisp currently sell for about twice as much as some varieties.

In response, a new "managed" or "club" system has emerged. The club's self-selected members pool funds to market a variety's trademarked brand name, limiting supply and the number of growers. The members' goal is to ensure high prices for high quality fruit. But the price is steep, and the club is exclusive. For the first time in its history, New England's medium-size to small orchards are restricted from growing certain new varieties for legal or financial, rather than horticultural, reasons.

Howgate Wonder

ORIGIN	DISCOVERED	RELEASED
England	1915	1932
PARENTAGE	**HARVEST**	**FLAVOR SCALE**
Blenheim Orange × Newton Wonder	Midseason	T 2 3 **4** S

Howgate Wonder is a very large, sweet, and juicy apple. It has a brownish red color over a yellow-green skin that becomes greasy in storage. Its crisp, cream-colored flesh is mildly tart. When used in cooking, it turns yellow, but it generally holds its shape. It is a good fresh-eating apple and outstanding in cider.

Noted for its size, Howgate Wonder held the unofficial title of world's largest apple in 2012, with one weighing in at 3 pounds 11 ounces. The prize apple was 7 inches across, with a 21-inch circumference.

Howgate Wonder was discovered in 1915 by G. Wratton, a retired policeman of Howgate Lane, Bembridge, Isle of Wight, and the original tree lived until the 1960s. It gets its large size from its Newton Wonder parent, an English apple from 1887, and its greasy skin from its other parent, Blenheim Orange, an English apple dating back to 1740.

Hubbardston Nonesuch | American Blush

ORIGIN		DISCOVERED	RELEASED
Hubbardston, Massachusetts		Early 1800s	
PARENTAGE		**HARVEST**	**FLAVOR SCALE**
unknown		Late season	T 2 3 **4** S

Hubbardston Nonesuch is a large apple with heavy red streaking on a yellow-green skin with occasional russeting. Its yellowish flesh is dense and juicy, and it has an unusually small core. It has a sweet, complex flavor good for cider and fresh eating, but it does not always translate well to cooking, and its flavor tends to fade in storage.

Early references to Hubbardston begin around 1832, and it enjoyed a period of considerable popularity throughout the Northeast for much of the 19th century. As late as 1905, Beach recommended Hubbardston for commercial orchards, but its growth habits are inconsistent, so it has never experienced widespread success despite its rich flavor.

Jersey Mac

ORIGIN		DISCOVERED	RELEASED
New Brunswick, New Jersey		1956	1971
PARENTAGE		**HARVEST**	**FLAVOR SCALE**
(Melba × [Wealthy × Starr]) × (Red Rome × Melba)		Early season	T **2** 3 4 S

Jersey Mac is a medium-size, round apple with a tough, dark red skin with green and red patches. Its tender, white flesh is mild and sweet, with hints of strawberry. It does not store well, but it can be used for both cooking and fresh eating. One grower calls Jersey Mac "a good choice for McIntosh lovers who are getting impatient waiting for the Macs to ripen."

Despite its name and resemblance to McIntosh, though, its complex parentage does not include that apple. It was developed at the Rutgers New Jersey Agricultural Experiment Station.

Jonagold

ORIGIN	DISCOVERED	RELEASED
Geneva, New York	1943	1968
PARENTAGE	HARVEST	FLAVOR SCALE
Jonathan × Golden Delicious	Midseason	T 2 3 **4** S

Jonagold is an outstanding apple that somehow has never caught on with the American public. It is a medium-size to large, conical apple with broad patches of red on a yellow skin. Jonagold's color is variable, but at its best it is a stunning combination of its parents, the rich, red Jonathan and Golden Delicious. Aromatic and very juicy, its light yellow flesh has a crisp, clean crunch reminiscent of Honeycrisp. Its flavor is mostly sweet, with a little tartness. An all-purpose apple, Jonagold's exceptional juiciness and flavor are especially good eaten fresh and pressed into cider.

Despite its outstanding flavor, texture, and beauty, to date Jonagolds have proven more popular around the globe than here in the United States, where it was developed at the New York State Agricultural Experiment Station. Its lack of commercial success notwithstanding—it is rarely found in supermarkets—this is one of the best apples introduced in the past 50 years.

Multicolored Apples

Karmijn de Sonnaville

ORIGIN	DISCOVERED	RELEASED
Netherlands	1949	1971
PARENTAGE	**HARVEST**	**FLAVOR SCALE**
Cox's Orange Pippin × Jonathan or Belle de Boskoop	Midseason	T 2 **3** 4 S

Karmijn de Sonnaville is a medium-size apple with complex flavor and coloring, with mingling shades of red, orange, yellow, and green. Its crisp, juicy flesh has a rich, spicy flavor nicely balanced between tart and sweet. It is outstanding for fresh eating and excellent in cider.

Karmijn was raised by Piet de Sonnaville on his family orchard in the central Netherlands. Like Jonagold, its exceptional flavor has not translated into commercial success in the United States, as it can be difficult to grow and lacks a user-friendly name.

Kearsarge

ORIGIN	DISCOVERED	RELEASED
Contoocook, New Hampshire	Age unknown	
PARENTAGE	**HARVEST**	**FLAVOR SCALE**
unknown	Midseason	T **2** 3 4 S

Kearsarge is a medium-size, round or boxy apple with red striping on a greenish yellow skin. Its cream-colored flesh is crisp and moderately juicy, and it has a mild, sweet flavor with hints of pear. It is good for both fresh eating and cooking.

Kearsarge is named for the mountain that dominates the view from Gould Hill Orchards, where the apple was discovered and where it is exclusively grown.

King of Tompkins County | King

ORIGIN	DISCOVERED	RELEASED
Warren County, New Jersey	Late 1700s	
PARENTAGE	**HARVEST**	**FLAVOR SCALE**
unknown	Midseason	T 2 **3** 4 S

King of Tompkins County is a large, round apple, crimson striped on a yellow skin. Its coarse, crisp, cream-colored flesh is aromatic and juicy, and its flavor is richly sweet with some tartness. It is especially good in applesauce and pies. It generally keeps well, and in storage it develops a naturally greasy skin.

King of Tompkins County might better be named King of Warren County, New Jersey, as that is where it was first grown. It was brought to Tompkins County, New York, in 1804 by Jacob Wycoff, and it enjoyed great popularity in the 1800s. In the early 1900s, it was still among the most widely grown apples in New York. But while the fruit is outstanding, the trees are difficult to grow, susceptible to disease and not very cold hardy.

The name King has been applied to several varieties; Tompkins County was added to distinguish this apple from others by that name.

Lady | Api, Christmas Apple

ORIGIN	DISCOVERED	RELEASED
France	1600s	
PARENTAGE	**HARVEST**	**FLAVOR SCALE**
unknown	Late season	**T** 2 3 4 S

Lady apple proves the adage that good things come in small packages. It is small but intense. Lady's red and green color varies depending on the amount of sunlight it gets; the green can lighten to yellow. Its bright white flesh is crisp and juicy, with hints of citrus.

While its small size makes Lady less than ideal for cooking, it is good

in salads, eaten fresh, and pickled, sweet or sour, in the latter case sometimes served with a hot sauce. Due to its small size, festive coloring, and ability to withstand a freeze, Lady is often featured in Christmas wreaths, and is also known as Christmas Apple. Lady is a brilliant sight in the orchard, cascading in thick clusters during late summer and fall.

Lady is one of the oldest known apple varieties, having been cultivated in France since the reign of Louis XIII. It may be even older, dating back to ancient Rome. It was one of the first European apples to be brought to America.

Lamb Abbey Pearmain

ORIGIN		DISCOVERED	RELEASED
England		1804	
PARENTAGE		**HARVEST**	**FLAVOR SCALE**
Newport Pippin × unknown		Midseason	T **2** 3 4 S

Lamb Abbey Pearmain is a medium-size to small, red-striped apple on a yellow skin, with outstanding flavor. Its yellow-white flesh is crisp and juicy. Its intense, sweet-tart taste has hints of pineapple. It is good for all purposes, and it stores well.

It was first grown by Mary Malcolm of the Lamb Abbey district of Dartford, Kent, from a Newtown Pippin seed, making it one of the first European apples to be developed from an American variety.

Macoun

ORIGIN		DISCOVERED	RELEASED
Geneva, New York		1909	1923
PARENTAGE		**HARVEST**	**FLAVOR SCALE**
McIntosh × Jersey Black		Midseason	T **2** 3 4 S

Few apples are as eagerly anticipated every fall in New England as Macoun. Macoun is predominantly red with green streaks, with an angular, boxy shape, distinguishing it from its McIntosh parent. It has a harder, crisper flesh than McIntosh, and its complex, sweet-tart flavor has hints of strawberry and spices. While good for most culinary uses, Macoun is one of the very best fresh-eating apples. It does not store as well as some varieties, another reason it is so coveted in the fall.

McIntosh supplies much of Macoun's flavor, juiciness, and bouquet. Macoun's other parent, Jersey Black, an American heirloom once known as Black Apple due to its dark color, gives Macoun its wine red tones and irregular shape.

Although developed by Richard Wellington at the New York State Agricultural Experiment Station, Macoun was named for Canadian pomologist William Tyrrell ("W. T.") Macoun. It is pronounced as if spelled "MacCowan," although some people say "MacCoon."

Maiden's Blush | Lady Blush, Maiden Blush, Red Cheek, Vestal

ORIGIN	DISCOVERED	RELEASED
Burlington, New Jersey	Late 1700s	
PARENTAGE	**HARVEST**	**FLAVOR SCALE**
unknown	Midseason	T **2** 3 4 S

Maiden's Blush is a medium-size to large apple with a red blush and light striping over greenish yellow skin. Its white flesh is crisp and juicy. It is tart and citrusy when first harvested, and it is best used for cooking, drying, and in cider and wine making. It mellows to a sweeter flavor over time and in storage.

Maiden's Blush was introduced by Samuel Allinson. It was once widely grown in America and was especially popular in Philadelphia in the early 1800s.

Multicolored Apples

Marshall McIntosh

ORIGIN		DISCOVERED	RELEASED
Fitchburg, Massachusetts		1967	
PARENTAGE		**HARVEST**	**FLAVOR SCALE**
McIntosh × unknown		Early season	T **2** 3 4 S

Marshall McIntosh is a medium-size, round apple with predominantly red skin and green highlights. Its bears a strong resemblance to its McIntosh parent for its tender flesh, juiciness, aroma, and sweet-tart flavor, but it has more red color and it ripens earlier than McIntosh.

Marshall McIntosh was discovered at Marshall Farms in Fitchburg, Massachusetts, but it was originally propagated by Roaring Brook Nurseries of Wales, Maine.

McIntosh

ORIGIN		DISCOVERED	RELEASED
Dundas County, Ontario, Canada		1801	1870
PARENTAGE		**HARVEST**	**FLAVOR SCALE**
Fameuse × Detroit Red		Midseason	T **2** 3 4 S

Although discovered in Canada, McIntosh is New England's leading apple, both in its own right (accounting for about two-thirds of the region's crop), and for its influence as a parent of several well-known New England varieties, especially Cortland, Empire, and Macoun. It has spawned several related varieties with the McIntosh name, including Early, Marshall, Rogers Red, and a newer addition with outstanding color and flavor, RubyMac.

McIntosh is a round, medium-size apple covered with uneven splashes of green and red. Its tender, white flesh is especially juicy, sweet-tart, and highly aromatic. McIntosh has been widely praised for its flavor, and it is outstanding for both fresh eating and cooking. It breaks down when cooked, making it a popular sauce apple. Its flavor is superb in pies and other baked goods, and it is often mixed with varieties with denser flesh for a firmer texture.

McIntosh bruises easily and does not store well. Its flavor and texture tend to become sweeter and creamier over time. But with the advent of controlled atmosphere (CA) storage and the growth regulator SmartFresh, crisp, tart McIntosh are now available throughout most of the year. If you bite into a mealy Mac today, chances are it was not kept refrigerated at the store or after it was purchased.

John McIntosh discovered the apple on his farm in southeastern Ontario, and the apple was nurtured and developed into commercial potential over the next few decades by his son.

McIntosh thrives in cold climates, needing the cool nights of late summer and early fall to produce apples with the greatest color and flavor, and the trees are hardy.

Apple breeders are continually trying to develop McIntosh with more red color, such as the sport strain Marshall. Two recent additions from the 1990s are Rogers McIntosh and RubyMac, the trademarked name of a variety discovered as a limb sport by Bernard Thome of Comstock Park, Michigan.

Melba

ORIGIN	DISCOVERED	RELEASED
Ottawa, Canada	1898	1909
PARENTAGE	**HARVEST**	**FLAVOR SCALE**
McIntosh × Liveland Raspberry	Early season	T **2** 3 4 S

Melba is yellow to lime green in color, with streaks and blushes of pink and red. Lightly sweet with a hint of tartness, Melba's fine, white flesh and thin skin give it a pleasing crispness, and it is good for both fresh eating and cooking.

Melba's parents are McIntosh and Liveland Raspberry. Also known as Lowland Raspberry or Red Cheek, Liveland Raspberry is an early-season apple that originated in the Lithuanian province of Lievland. Now rare, it was introduced to the United States in 1883. While McIntosh contributes to Melba's fragrant, sweet-tart flavor, Liveland Raspberry influences its early ripeness and supplies its tender flesh and thin skin.

It was developed by W. T. Macoun at the Central Experiment Farm in Ottawa, Canada.

Melrose

ORIGIN	DISCOVERED	RELEASED
Wooster, Ohio	1944	
PARENTAGE	**HARVEST**	**FLAVOR SCALE**
Jonathan × Red Delicious	Midseason	T 2 3 **4** S

Melrose is a large, round, yellow-green apple overlaid in red, with occasional russeting. Its coarse, crisp, white flesh is juicy, and its tart flavor with a touch of sweetness improves over time. It is a good cooking apple, as it keeps its shape, and it stores reasonably well.

The official state apple of Ohio, Melrose was discovered by Freeman S. Howlett at the Ohio Agricultural Experiment Station. It is not to be confused with another apple of the same name, also known as White Melrose, a yellowish apple attributed to the monks of Melrose Abbey, Scotland, around 1830.

Milton

ORIGIN	DISCOVERED	RELEASED
Geneva, New York	1909	1923
PARENTAGE	**HARVEST**	**FLAVOR SCALE**
McIntosh × Yellow Transparent	Early season	T 2 **3** 4 S

Milton is round-flat, medium-size, and red over green skin, with prominent white lenticels. Its tender white flesh is aromatic and juicy, sweet with some tartness. It does not store well.

Milton was developed by Richard Wellington at the New York State Agricultural Experiment Station and named for a small village in Ulster County, New York.

Mollie's Delicious

ORIGIN	DISCOVERED	RELEASED
New Brunswick, New Jersey	1948	1966
PARENTAGE	**HARVEST**	**FLAVOR SCALE**
(Golden Delicious × Edgewood) × (Red Gravenstein × Close)	Early season	T 2 3 **4** S

Mollie's Delicious is large, ribbed, and angular or conical in shape, with red coloring over a yellow skin. Its cream-colored flesh is crisp, coarse, and juicy, and its flavor is sweet with hints of citrus. It tends to bruise easily, but it can be stored for several months.

Mollie's Delicious was developed at the Rutgers New Jersey Agricultural Experiment Station, and it was named after an admirer of the apple, Mollie Whatley.

Opalescent | Hudson's Pride of Michigan

ORIGIN	DISCOVERED	RELEASED
Barry County, Michigan	1880	
PARENTAGE	**HARVEST**	**FLAVOR SCALE**
Golden Delicious × Newtown Pippin	Midseason	T 2 3 **4** S

Opalescent is a large apple with red overlaid on a yellow skin, with prominent white lenticels. Its coarse, yellow flesh is moderately juicy, and its mild flavor is mostly sweet, with a little tartness. It is similar to Twenty Ounce in appearance, but its flavor is not as good, and it does not store well.

Once widely grown in New England, Opalescent was discovered by George Hudson, who originally named it Hudson's Pride of Michigan. It

was renamed when it was commercially released in 1880. Some sources trace its release to Xenia, Ohio, in 1899.

Rambour Franc | Summer Rambo

ORIGIN		DISCOVERED		RELEASED
Picardy, France		1530s		
PARENTAGE		**HARVEST**		**FLAVOR SCALE**
unknown		Early season		T 2 **3** 4 S

Rambour Franc is a large, yellow-green apple with pink to red striping. Its yellow-green flesh is moderately crisp and juicy, and it has a balanced, though mild, sweet-tart flavor. It is good for both fresh eating and cooking, especially in pies. It does not keep well.

It is one of the oldest known apples, first grown in the village of Rembures, around 1530. It was first cited growing in America in 1665.

Reine de Reinette | Golden Winter Pearmain, King of the Pippins, Reinette of the Crown, Queen of the Pippins

ORIGIN		DISCOVERED		RELEASED
France		1770		
PARENTAGE		**HARVEST**		**FLAVOR SCALE**
unknown		Midseason		T 2 **3** 4 S

Reine de Reinette is a large, boxy red apple with a green blush and occasional russeting. Its crisp white flesh is moderately juicy, and it has a slightly tart, nutty flavor. It is good for both fresh eating and cooking, and it keeps well.

Reine de Reinette's origin is uncertain, but it probably is from northern Europe. By some accounts, it was discovered in Holland and named Kroon Renet (Reinette of the Crown). After migrating to France, the apple was renamed Reine de Reinette. It may have been introduced in England around the same time and given the name Golden Winter Pearmain.

English growers eventually realized that Golden Winter Pearmain was identical with Reine de Reinette, and renamed the apple King of the Pippins. To further confuse matters, Reine de Reinette was imported to England from France and renamed Queen of the Pippins.

All of these names refer to the same apple.

Ribston Pippin | Ribston

ORIGIN	DISCOVERED	RELEASED
Yorkshire, England	Early 1700s	
PARENTAGE	HARVEST	FLAVOR SCALE
unknown	Midseason	T **2** 3 4 S

Ribston Pippin is as striking to behold as it is good to eat. A small to medium-size, slightly conical apple, its color ranges from brown to gold, orange and crimson. It is aromatic, and its complex flavor, more tart than sweet at harvest, becomes spicy and sweet in storage, with hints of pear. Its yellow flesh is crisp and juicy. It is outstanding for fresh eating and good for cooking. While its flavor improves in storage, it does not keep long.

Ribston Pippin became popular in New England, New York, and parts of Canada in the early 1800s. It is parent to England's most well-known apple, Cox's Orange Pippin.

Smokehouse | English Vandevere, Red Vandevere

ORIGIN		DISCOVERED	RELEASED
Lancaster County, Pennsylvania		1848	
PARENTAGE		**HARVEST**	**FLAVOR SCALE**
Vandevere × unknown		Late season	T **2** 3 4 S

Smokehouse is a medium-size to large, round apple, mostly red with yellow highlights. Its cream-colored flesh is moderately crisp and juicy. Its flavor is mostly sweet with a mild tartness, lacking distinction. It is primarily a fresh eating apple.

The variety originated on the farm of William Gibbons, who named it for its proximity to his smokehouse. Smokehouse closely resembles Vandevere, a Maryland variety from 1806 presumed to be one of Smokehouse's parents.

Snow | Fameuse

ORIGIN		DISCOVERED	RELEASED
Canada		1730	
PARENTAGE		**HARVEST**	**FLAVOR SCALE**
unknown		Late season	T **2** 3 4 S

Snow is a small to medium-size, red apple with green and pink striping. Its name comes from its white flesh, which is sometimes stained red beneath its skin. Snow is a crisp, juicy, aromatic apple, sweet-tart with a slight strawberry flavor. Snow is outstanding for both fresh eating and cider. It does not store well.

While it is a fine apple, Snow's main legacy is as a parent to McIntosh. Snow gives McIntosh its thin skin, white flesh, and some of its sweet-tart flavor. McIntosh inherited Snow's ability to thrive in cold climates, needing the cool nights of late summer and early fall to produce apples with the greatest color and flavor.

Snow's origins are unclear, but it is a very old apple. It may have originated in France rather than Canada, eventually migrating south to the United States. It was reported growing in Vermont's Champlain Valley in the early 1600s.

Spencer

ORIGIN	DISCOVERED	RELEASED
Summerland, British Columbia	1926	1959
PARENTAGE	**HARVEST**	**FLAVOR SCALE**
McIntosh × Golden Delicious	Midseason	T 2 3 **4** S

Spencer is conical, and nearly solid red-pink in color, with some green highlights. Its flesh is crisp, juicy, and sweet, but less so than its Golden Delicious parent. It is good for both fresh eating and cooking, especially for pies and sauce. Spencers are not noted for a lengthy storage life, so enjoy them close to harvest in mid-October.

Spencer was developed by R. C. Palmer at Canada's Pacific Agri-Food Research Centre.

Multicolored Apples

Spigold | Spygold

ORIGIN		DISCOVERED	RELEASED
Geneva, New York		1943	1962
PARENTAGE		HARVEST	FLAVOR SCALE
Red Spy × Golden Delicious		Midseason	T 2 3 **4** S

Spigold is a large, round or boxy, yellow-green apple with red streaks and prominent white lenticels. Its cream-colored flesh is crisp and juicy. It has spicy flavor, more sweet than tart. Its thin skin bruises easily, and it keeps for about three months.

Despite its outstanding flavor, due to its large size and its tendency to bruise, Spigold is a better apple for processing than for shipping. It was developed at the New York State Agricultural Experiment Station.

Suncrisp

ORIGIN	DISCOVERED	RELEASED
New Brunswick, New Jersey	1990s	
PARENTAGE	HARVEST	FLAVOR SCALE
Golden Delicious Cox's × (Orange Pippin × Cortland)	Late season	T **2** 3 4 S

Suncrisp is a large yellow apple with orange-red striping. Its cream-colored flesh is crisp, juicy, and sweet-tart when first picked. It becomes sweeter and develops a complex, spicy flavor in storage, where it can keep for up to six months. It is especially good for cooking.

Suncrisp was developed by Dr. Frederick Hough at the Rutgers New Jersey Agricultural Experiment Station, and its name is trademarked by Rutgers University.

Multicolored Apples

Twenty Ounce | Cayuga Red Streak, Eighteen Ounce, Wine

ORIGIN	DISCOVERED	RELEASED
unknown	1840s	
PARENTAGE	**HARVEST**	**FLAVOR SCALE**
unknown	Midseason	T **2** 3 4 S

Twenty Ounce is a very large, heavy, yellow-green apple with orange and red highlights and little bumps on its skin. It. Its coarse, cream-colored flesh is crisp, juicy, and more tart than sweet. It is better as a cooking than fresh eating apple, and it has a fairly short storage life.

The origin of Twenty Ounce is unclear, but it is thought to have originated in either Connecticut or New York. Its popularity once extended from New England to Maryland. It is not to be confused with Twenty Ounce Pippin.

Vermont Gold

ORIGIN	DISCOVERED	RELEASED
Vermont	1980s	
PARENTAGE	**HARVEST**	**FLAVOR SCALE**
unknown	Late season	T 2 **3** 4 S

Vermont Gold is a small to medium-size, round apple with pale yellow skin and a pink blush. Its tender white flesh is juicy and has a nicely balanced, sweet-tart flavor. Its exceptionally thin skin gives the variety an unusual texture, but it is highly susceptible to bruising, making it difficult to handle and ship.

Vermont Gold was developed and patented by William Luginbuhl, a pathologist and former dean of the University of Vermont College of Medicine, and a passionate amateur horticulturist. He offered ten trees to any grower in Vermont who wanted them, but only a few accepted.

Multicolored Apples

Vista Bella

ORIGIN		DISCOVERED	RELEASED
New Brunswick, New Jersey		1956	1974
July Red, Melba, Sonora, Starr, Williams		Early season	T **2** 3 4 S

Vista Bella is a small to medium-size, round apple, red with a green blush. Its white flesh is moderately juicy, with mildly tart flavor and hints of raspberry. Its main distinction is that it ripens as early as the end of July. Like most early-season apples, Vista Bella is best eaten soon after it is picked, as it does not keep well.

Vista Bella was developed at the Rutgers New Jersey Agricultural Experiment Station. It got its name because it grew well in trials in the Guatemalan highlands.

Wagener

ORIGIN	DISCOVERED	RELEASED
New York	1791	1847
PARENTAGE	**HARVEST**	**FLAVOR SCALE**
Siberian Crab × unknown	Midseason	T **2** 3 4 S

Wagener is a boxy apple, mostly a rich red with yellow or green highlights. It has crisp, juicy, cream-colored flesh, and has a lively sweet-tart flavor. It is good for fresh eating and cooking, and it keeps well. The trees are hardy, but short-lived and difficult to grow.

No longer widely grown, Wagener's legacy continues as a parent of Idared.

Wagener was originally grown by George Wheeler in the village of Penn Yan in New York's Finger Lakes region, from seeds he brought with him from Dutchess County, New York. Abraham Wagener bought Wheeler's farm in 1796 and gave the apple its name.

Wealthy

ORIGIN	DISCOVERED	RELEASED
Excelsior, Minnesota	1861	1868
PARENTAGE	**HARVEST**	**FLAVOR SCALE**
Cherry Crab × unknown	Midseason	T 2 **3** 4 S

Wealthy is a midwestern variety produced from a crab apple seed from New England. It is a medium-size apple, strawberry red and light green. Its crisp, aromatic white flesh is sometimes stained red, and it is juicy, with a lively sweet-tart flavor. It is good for both cooking and fresh eating. The trees are exceptionally hardy.

In 1853, Peter Gideon moved to Minnesota and began experimenting with apple growing, planting thousands of trees. Most died within a few years in its harsh climate, and none bore much fruit. With dwindling funds, Gideon purchased a bushel of cherry crab apple seeds from Albert Emerson of Bangor, Maine, in 1861. Through his determination, one of these seeds eventually produced the apple that Gideon then named after his wife, Wealthy (Hull) Gideon.

Westfield Seek-No-Further | Connecticut Seek-No-Further

ORIGIN	DISCOVERED	RELEASED
Westfield, Massachusetts	1700s	
PARENTAGE	**HARVEST**	**FLAVOR SCALE**
unknown	Midseason	T 2 3 **4** S

Westfield Seek-No-Further is a round apple with dull cherry coloring over a yellow skin, with prominent lenticels and patches of russet. Its aromatic white flesh is crisp and moderately juicy, and its flavor more sweet than tart, with hints of pear. It is best as a fresh eating apple. The trees, while hardy, grow unpredictably from region to region.

The name Seek-No-Further was applied to several apples besides the Westfield Seek-No-Further, which is believed to date back to at least the

Revolutionary War. It first spread from western Massachusetts south to Connecticut, and was cited in Ohio in 1796.

Westfield Seek-No-Further was popular in parts of the Northeast during much of the 19th century. An 1846 report by the New York State Agricultural Society called it "a truly excellent apple" originating in Westfield, "or its neighborhood, a beautiful meadow town, about ten miles west of Springfield, in the Connecticut Valley, in Massachusetts. For many miles up and down, and round about that river, it is the apple par excellence. . . . Whole orchards are planted of this fruit, and nowhere does it flourish in higher luxuriance and perfection."

Wolf River

ORIGIN		DISCOVERED	RELEASED
Fremont, Wisconsin		1875	
PARENTAGE		**HARVEST**	**FLAVOR SCALE**
Alexander × unknown		Midseason	T 2 **3** 4 S

Wolf River is a large, bulky apple, often lopsided and exceeding one pound. Its pale yellow skin is covered in red. Its coarse flesh is juicy, with mildly tart flavor. It is best used in cooking and in cider. It does not store well. Its main virtues other than its size are that its trees are hardy and they are disease resistant.

Wolf River was discovered on the farm of W. A. Springer along the river that gave it its name. It closely resembles and is probably a seedling of the Russian apple Alexander.

York | York Imperial

ORIGIN	DISCOVERED	RELEASED
York, Pennsylvania	Early 1800s	
PARENTAGE	**HARVEST**	**FLAVOR SCALE**
unknown	Midseason	T 2 **3** 4 S

York is a medium-size to large, somewhat lopsided apple with red streaks covering a green skin. It has crisp, yellow flesh, and is moderately juicy. Its sweet-tart flavor mellows over time to a milder, sweeter apple. It is good for both fresh eating and cooking, but it is most highly prized as a processing apple due to its yellow flesh, which adds color to sauce and pies, and its small core size. It is an excellent keeper.

It is not widely grown in New England, but it is popular in Virginia and Pennsylvania, its state of origin.

Zestar! | Zesta

ORIGIN	DISCOVERED	RELEASED
Minnesota	1999	
PARENTAGE	**HARVEST**	**FLAVOR SCALE**
State Fair × MN1691	Early season	T 2 3 **4** S

Zestar! is a medium-size, round, mostly red apple over a yellow base. Its white flesh is crisp and juicy, and more sweet than tart. A good all-purpose apple, its flavor and texture make Zestar! one of the best of the new, early-season varieties, though it browns easily and stores well for only a few weeks.

Zestar! is the trademarked name for the variety developed at the University of Minnesota Agricultural Experiment Station.

Akane | Tokyo Rose, Prime Red

ORIGIN	DISCOVERED	RELEASED
Japan	1937	1970
PARENTAGE	**HARVEST**	**FLAVOR SCALE**
Jonathan × Worcester Pearmain	Early season	T 2 **3** 4 S

Akane (ah-KAH-neh) is also known as Tokyo Rose and Prime Red in its native Japan, and Primrouge in France for its striking red color. It is more than pretty to look at, though. It has sweet-tart flavor with hints of strawberry, crisp white flesh, and lots of juice. One of the best early-season apples, it is considered good for baking as well as for fresh eating, as it holds its shape well.

Akane has a cosmopolitan pedigree: a Japanese apple resulting from a cross between the English heirloom Worcester Pearmain, known for its strawberry flavor, and Jonathan, an American heirloom with outstanding flavor and distinctive red color.

Alexander | Aporta

ORIGIN	DISCOVERED	RELEASED
Ukraine	1700s	
PARENTAGE	**HARVEST**	**FLAVOR SCALE**
unknown	Midseason	T 2 3 **4** S

Alexander is a large, sweet-tart, juicy apple with a red-orange blush on a pale yellow skin. Its crisp white flesh has a hint of yellow. Alexander is best used in cooking, although it is also good eaten fresh. It does not store well.

Alexander is still grown by its original name, Aporta, in parts of Kazakhstan, where the modern apple originated, and where there still are primeval forests of wild apple trees of every shape and size, bursting with genetic material.

The apple was renamed in honor of Czar Alexander I (1777–1825).

It arrived in England in 1817, and it was introduced in America by the Massachusetts Horticultural Society between 1830 and 1835, with three other eastern European varieties, Duchess of Oldenburg, Red Astrachan, and Tetofsky.

Arkansas Black | Arkansas Black Twig

ORIGIN	DISCOVERED	RELEASED
Northwest Arkansas	1842	1870
PARENTAGE	**HARVEST**	**FLAVOR SCALE**
Winesap × unknown	Late season	T **2** 3 4 S

Arkansas Black is a round, deep red, conical apple with heavy skin and dense, cream-colored flesh. It has a spicy flavor, more tart than sweet. It is widely used for processing and cider making. It is an excellent keeper, and its skin naturally darkens in storage.

There are conflicting reports about Arkansas Black's origins, although both stories trace the apple to Arkansas's northwest corner. One account attributes it to Mr. Brattwait of Benton County, while another claims it was discovered on the farm of John Crawford in Washington County. It was introduced around 1870.

Arkansas Black is distinct from Arkansas and Mammoth Black Twig.

Black Oxford

ORIGIN	DISCOVERED	RELEASED
Oxford County, Maine	About 1790	
PARENTAGE	**HARVEST**	**FLAVOR SCALE**
unknown	Late season	T 2 **3** 4 S

Black Oxford is Maine's most famous apple, although it is little known or grown beyond New England. A medium-size, roundish apple named for its distinctive dark, purple-red skin, it has green highlights and prominent white lenticels. Its dense white flesh has a hint of green, and is only

moderately juicy. Its sweet-tart flavor is good for all purposes, especially in pies and cider. Its flavor becomes sweeter and more complex in storage, and its storage life is exceptional.

According to George Stilphen, author of *The Apples of Maine,* Black Oxford "was found as a seedling by Nathaniel Haskell on the farm of one Valentine, a nail maker and farmer of Paris in Oxford County, about 1790 and the original tree was still standing in 1907, the farm being then owned by John Swett."

Blue Pearmain

ORIGIN	DISCOVERED	RELEASED
New England	1800s	
PARENTAGE	**HARVEST**	**FLAVOR SCALE**
unknown	Late season	T **2** 3 4 S

Blue Pearmain is a large, round, boxy apple that gets its name from its dark plum-colored bloom (the natural, protective wax that covers an apple). Its red and green skin has a rough, speckled appearance, and it is a little chewy. Its tender, green-tinged white flesh is moderately juicy. Its flavor is sweet and bland with a trace of bitterness. Used mostly in cider and for cooking, it is not considered a good keeper, although the trees are hardy.

Blue Pearmain is of uncertain origin, but it has been grown for at least two centuries in much of New England, particularly in higher elevations. It was so well known in the 1830s that Edward Sayer wrote that to describe it "would be useless." It was first cited by William Kenrick in 1833, who wrote that it was popular near Boston.

Braeburn

ORIGIN	DISCOVERED	RELEASED
Nelson, New Zealand	1952	
PARENTAGE	**HARVEST**	**FLAVOR SCALE**
Lady Hamilton × unknown	Late season	T 2 **3** 4 S

Braeburn is a slightly conical, crimson red apple overlaid on thin, yellow skin. Its yellow flesh is dense, aromatic, and juicy, and it has sweet-tart flavor with a hint of citrus. Braeburn is good for both fresh eating and cooking, and it has three to four times as much vitamin C as the average apple. It keeps well in storage. Although it was widely planted through the 1990s, its popularity appears to have peaked.

Braeburn was discovered on the farm of O. Moran and named for the apple's first commercial distributor, Braeburn Orchard. It is probably a seedling of Lady Hamilton; by some accounts, it is a cross of Lady Hamilton with Granny Smith.

Burgundy

ORIGIN	DISCOVERED	RELEASED
Geneva, New York	1953	1974
PARENTAGE	**HARVEST**	**FLAVOR SCALE**
(Monroe × NY18491) × (Macoun × Antonovka)	Early season	T **2** 3 4 S

Burgundy is a medium-size to large, dark red apple, round and oblate, with occasional light streaking. Its cream-colored flesh is crisp and juicy. It has sweet-tart flavor similar to that of its parent Macoun, and like Macoun it does not store very well.

Its name refers to the rich, red color of Burgundy wine, and it was developed by Robert Lamb and Roger D. Way at the New York State Agricultural Experiment Station.

Chenango | Chenango Strawberry

ORIGIN	DISCOVERED	RELEASED
Chenango, New York	1800s	
PARENTAGE	**HARVEST**	**FLAVOR SCALE**
Midseason	Early	T 2 3 **4** S

Chenango is a medium-size, conical apple, mostly rich red in color over pale yellow skin. Its tender, white flesh is aromatic, sweet but mild, with hints of strawberry. It is good for both fresh eating and cooking, but it does not store well.

Its history is unknown. It may have originated in New York's Madison County, or it may have come to Chenango County from Connecticut. According to Beach, it dates back to at least 1850.

Chinook

ORIGIN	DISCOVERED	RELEASED
Summerland, British Columbia	2000	
PARENTAGE	**HARVEST**	**FLAVOR SCALE**
Splendour × Gala	Late season	T **2** 3 4 S

Chinook is a small- to medium-size, slightly conical apple, mostly pink-red over yellow-green skin. Its flesh is aromatic, crisp, and juicy, and it has outstanding, sweet-tart flavor. It keeps well.

Although both its Gala and Splendour parents reach good size, Chinook's small fruit has so far limited its commercial success. It was developed at Canada's Pacific Agri-Food Research Centre.

Connell Red | Fireside

ORIGIN	DISCOVERED	RELEASED
Minnesota	1943	
PARENTAGE	**HARVEST**	**FLAVOR SCALE**
McIntosh × Longfield	Late season	T 2 3 4 **S**

Connell Red is a medium-size to large, round apple, mostly red over a yellow skin. Its crisp, white flesh is highly aromatic, with a rich, sweet flavor. It keeps well, and its skin develops a natural greasiness in storage. The trees are hardy.

Fireside was developed at the Minnesota Agricultural Experiment Station of the University of Minnesota. Technically Connell Red is a sport of Fireside, although they are classified as the same variety. Several midwestern growers also found the red Fireside strain in their orchards in the late 1940s, but Tom Connell of Menomonie, Wisconsin, named and patented Connell Red in 1956. This was seen by some as a breach of apple-naming etiquette, which favors a name that mentions the tree's lineage, such as Fireside Red, rather than an individual.

CrimsonCrisp

ORIGIN	DISCOVERED	RELEASED
Cream Ridge, New Jersey	1971	2005
PARENTAGE	**HARVEST**	**FLAVOR SCALE**
Crandal, Edgewood, Golden Delicious, Rome, Jonathan, Melba, and others	Midseason	T 2 3 **4** S

CrimsonCrisp, as its name implies, is a deep red–purple apple with occasional yellow highlights. Its crispy yellow flesh has sweet-tart flavor. It is an all-purpose apple that is best eaten fresh. It resists apple scab, and it stores well.

CrimsonCrisp was developed by PRI, the joint apple-breeding program of Purdue University, Rutgers University, and the University of Illi-

nois. The first seedlings were grown at the Rutgers Fruit Research and Development Center, and developed at the Purdue University Horticultural Research farm in West Lafayette, Indiana. Its complex parentage includes eight named varieties, including Golden Delicious, and several numbered ones.

Davey

ORIGIN		DISCOVERED	RELEASED
North Grafton, Massachusetts		1928	1950
PARENTAGE		HARVEST	FLAVOR SCALE
McIntosh × unknown		Midseason	T 2 **3** 4 S

Davey (rhymes with "savvy") is mostly red with occasional light yellow striping and prominent greenish lenticels. Like its McIntosh parent, Davey is juicy, with nicely balanced sweet-tart flavor. Its flavor and texture have also been compared to Baldwin, with a hint of strawberry. Its white flesh is crisper and it stores better than McIntosh.

Davey was discovered by Stearns Lothrop Davenport of Creeper Hill in North Grafton. As secretary of the Worcester County Horticultural Society, Davenport is credited with preserving more than 60 heirloom apple varieties.

Enterprise

ORIGIN		DISCOVERED	RELEASED
West Lafayette, Indiana		1978	1990
PARENTAGE		HARVEST	FLAVOR SCALE
Golden Delicious, McIntosh, Rome Beauty, and others		Late season	T **2** 3 4 S

Enterprise is a round, medium-size to large, deep red apple with white lenticels. Its crisp flesh at harvest becomes tender in storage. Its spicy, sweet-tart flavor is best for cooking. Its skin is a little chewy and becomes waxy in storage, but it keeps exceptionally well.

Developed for disease resistance by Edwin B. Williams of PRI, the joint apple-breeding program of Purdue University, Rutgers University, and the University of Illinois, Enterprise is immune to apple scab and highly resistant to fire blight and cedar apple rust.

Esopus Spitzenburg

ORIGIN		DISCOVERED	RELEASED
Esopus, New York		1700s	
PARENTAGE		HARVEST	FLAVOR SCALE
unknown		Late season	T 2 3 **4** S

Esopus Spitzenburg is a tall, conical, red apple with light yellow lenticels. Its pale yellow flesh is crisp and juicy. Its outstanding, spicy flavor is more sweet than tart, and it becomes more complex as it ages. It is a good all-purpose apple, especially good in pies. It stores well.

Its origins are unclear, but it dates to at least 1790, and it was widely planted across the United States in the 19th century. President Thomas Jefferson, an accomplished horticulturist, grew many apples on his Monticello plantation in Charlottesville, Virginia (an outstanding preservation orchard is maintained there today), and Esopus was one of his favorites. Writer Washington Irving also had a well-known fondness for Spitzenburgs.

Freedom

ORIGIN		DISCOVERED	RELEASED
Geneva, New York		1958	1983
PARENTAGE		**HARVEST**	**FLAVOR SCALE**
Golden Delicious, Macoun, Rome, and Antonovka, among others		Late season	T **2** 3 4 S

Freedom is a large, oblate, round apple with red striping over yellow skin. Its cream-colored flesh is crisp and juicy with sweet-tart flavor. An all-purpose apple, it is good for fresh eating, sauce, and cider. It stores well.

Developed for disease resistance at the New York State Agricultural Experiment Station, its parentage includes Golden Delicious, Macoun, Rome, and a Russian apple, Antonovka. Its name refers to its "freedom" from apple scab.

Hampshire

ORIGIN		DISCOVERED	RELEASED
Contoocook, New Hampshire		1978	1990
PARENTAGE		**HARVEST**	**FLAVOR SCALE**
unknown		Late season	T **2** 3 4 S

Hampshire is a large apple, nearly solid red, with crisp, juicy, cream-colored flesh. A McIntosh-like apple, it is aromatic and has thin, chewy skin and mild, sweet-tart flavor. It is good for both fresh eating and cooking. It keeps well.

Hampshire is a chance seedling discovered by Erick Leadbeater, then owner of Gould Hill Farm, in a block containing several varieties, including Cortland, McIntosh, and Red Delicious.

Holly

ORIGIN	DISCOVERED	RELEASED
Ohio	1952	1970
PARENTAGE	**HARVEST**	**FLAVOR SCALE**
Jonathan × Red Delicious	Late season	T 2 3 **4** S

Holly is a large, conical or boxy apple, with rich, pink-red color over a yellow skin. Its cream-colored flesh is crisp and juicy. A sweet apple like its Red Delicious parent, it has a little tartness. It is an all-purpose apple and a good keeper.

Holly was developed by the Ohio Agricultural Research and Development Center.

Idared

ORIGIN	DISCOVERED	RELEASED
Moscow, Idaho	(1935)	1942
PARENTAGE	**HARVEST**	**FLAVOR SCALE**
Jonathan × Wagener	Late season	T **2** 3 4 S

Idared is a large, round apple with a chewy, ruby-red skin. Its crisp flesh is white with a greenish tinge. Its flavor is somewhat tart and unremarkable when first picked, but it develops sweetness and complexity and becomes juicier over time. After a few weeks or even months in cold storage, it is a superb apple for sauce, pies (it holds its shape when cooked), and cider.

Idared was developed by Leif Verner, head of the Department of Horticulture at the Idaho Agricultural Experiment Station.

Jonamac

ORIGIN	DISCOVERED	RELEASED
Geneva, New York	1944	1972
PARENTAGE	**HARVEST**	**FLAVOR SCALE**
Jonathan × McIntosh	Early season	T 2 3 **4** S

Jonamac is a medium-size, round, McIntosh-type apple, mostly deep red over pale yellow-green skin. Its skin is thin but chewy, and its aromatic white flesh is tender. Its tart flavor is similar to that of McIntosh, but a little sweeter, with a hint of strawberry. It ripens before McIntosh, and it does not store well.

Names for the apple were solicited before it was introduced, and more than 500 entries were submitted. Two of the seven people suggesting the winning name Jonamac were New Englanders: William Darrow Sr. of Green Mountain Orchards in Putney, Vermont, and Rockwood Berry, former executive director of the New York-New England Apple Institute, now the New England Apple Association.

Jonamac was developed by Roger D. Way at the New York State Agricultural Experiment Station.

Jonared

ORIGIN	DISCOVERED	RELEASED
Peshastin, Washington	1930	1934
PARENTAGE	**HARVEST**	**FLAVOR SCALE**
A sport variety of Jonathan	Midseason	T **2** 3 4 S

Jonared resembles its parent, Jonathan, but it has brighter red coloring over yellow skin, and it ripens a little earlier. Jonared has Jonathan's crisp, juicy flesh and sweet-tart flavor, and it is good eaten fresh and is outstanding in cider and pies.

It was discovered on the farm of W. Uecher.

Jonathan

ORIGIN	DISCOVERED	RELEASED
Ulster County, New York	Early 1800s	
PARENTAGE	**HARVEST**	**FLAVOR SCALE**
Esopus Spitzenburg × unknown	Late season	T 2 **3** 4 S

Jonathan is a medium-size, conical apple with a bright red skin over pale yellow. Its whitish flesh is aromatic, crisp, and juicy, and it has a spicy, tangy flavor. Applesauce made with Jonathan turns pink from its red skin color, and it is especially good in cooking, although its shape does not hold for baked apples. It has a relatively short storage life.

First described in 1826, the variety originated on the farm of Philip Rick, in Woodstock, New York. Its name commemorates Jonathan Hasbrouck, who spotted the apple growing in brush on Rick's farm.

While not widely grown in New England, Jonathan remains popular in the Midwest.

Keepsake

ORIGIN	DISCOVERED	RELEASED
Minnesota	1978	
PARENTAGE	**HARVEST**	**FLAVOR SCALE**
Frostbite × Northern Spy	Late season	T 2 3 **4** S

Keepsake is an irregularly shaped, mostly red apple over a yellow skin. Its light yellow flesh is dense and juicy, and it has a sweet, spicy flavor. It is good for fresh eating and cooking. The trees are hardy, and it keeps well, storing up to six months.

Keepsake was developed at the Minnesota Agricultural Experiment Station of the University of Minnesota. It is a sibling of Sweet Sixteen, and both apples gain a complex sweetness from their Frostbite parent. Frostbite, which was only introduced in 2008, has flavor that has been compared to molasses or sugar cane.

Still a relatively new variety, Keepsake has already had a tremendous impact as the only known parent of Honeycrisp.

Liberty

ORIGIN		DISCOVERED	RELEASED
Geneva, New York		1978	
PARENTAGE		HARVEST	FLAVOR SCALE
Macoun × Purdue		Midseason	T 2 **3** 4 S

Liberty is a medium-size, slightly conical, mostly red apple overlaid on yellow skin. Its crisp, cream-colored flesh is often tinged pink, and it is moderately juicy. It has a nicely balanced, sweet-tart flavor. Liberty is resistant to such common diseases as apple scab, cedar apple rust, fire blight, and mildew.

Liberty was developed by Robert Lamb at the New York State Agricultural Experiment Station.

Monroe

ORIGIN		DISCOVERED	RELEASED
Geneva, New York		1910	1949
PARENTAGE		HARVEST	FLAVOR SCALE
Jonathan × Rome Beauty		Late season	T 2 3 **4** S

Monroe is a medium-size, round, red apple over a yellow skin. Its tender, cream-colored flesh is more sweet than tart, and moderately juicy. It is a good fresh-eating apple, and it is an especially good cider apple. It stores well.

It grows well in parts of New England, especially Vermont, and its popularity peaked in the 1960s. Named for Monroe County, it was developed by Richard Wellington at the New York State Agricultural Experiment Station.

Northern Spy

ORIGIN	DISCOVERED	RELEASED
Salisbury, Connecticut	1800	1840
PARENTAGE	**HARVEST**	**FLAVOR SCALE**
unknown	Midseason	T 2 **3** 4 S

Northern Spy is one of New England's oldest and best-known apples. It is a large, angular apple with a distinctive, pink-red shade. Its sweet-tart flavor is spicy and complex, and it is good for both fresh eating and cooking. It is an especially good pie apple.

In his 1905 classic, *The Apples of New York*, S. A. Beach is effusive about Northern Spy. Comparing it to Baldwin and Rhode Island Greening, Beach writes that Northern Spy "is superior to either of these in flavor and quality. . . . The flesh is very juicy, crisp, tender, and most excellent for either dessert or culinary uses."

It is one of several varieties discovered by Heman Chapin, grown from seeds he took with him from Salisbury, Connecticut, to East Bloomfield, New York. Northern Spy was introduced 40 years later.

Nova | Nova Spy

ORIGIN	DISCOVERED	RELEASED
Kentville, Nova Scotia	1986	
PARENTAGE	**HARVEST**	**FLAVOR SCALE**
Nova Easygro × (Red Spy × Golden Delicious)	Late season	T 2 3 **4** S

Nova is medium-size, round, mostly red with a little yellow striping. Its tender, whitish flesh is sweet and juicy, with a little tartness. Its flavor is similar to that of Northern Spy, and it is good for fresh eating, cooking, and cider. The trees are disease resistant, and the apples store well.

Nova Spy was developed by Canada's Atlantic Food and Horticulture Research Centre.

PaulaRed

ORIGIN		DISCOVERED	RELEASED
Sparta Township, Michigan		1960	1968
PARENTAGE		HARVEST	FLAVOR SCALE
unknown		Early season	T **2** 3 4 S

PaulaRed is a striking red color with occasional light yellow or green striping and prominent white lenticels. PaulaRed's tender white flesh is sweet-tart, with a hint of strawberry. It is good for both cooking and fresh eating, and it is slow to brown, making it good in salads. One of the first apples of the New England season, PaulaRed is not available for long and should be eaten soon after picking, as it does not store well.

PaulaRed was discovered by grower Lewis Arends from a chance seedling near a block of McIntosh trees, and named after Arends's wife, Pauline. Its sweet-tart flavor and two-toned color suggest PaulaRed may have McIntosh in its parentage.

Pink Lady | Cripps Pink

ORIGIN		DISCOVERED	RELEASED
Australia		1970s	1989
PARENTAGE		HARVEST	FLAVOR SCALE
Golden Delicious × Lady Williams		Late season	T **2** 3 4 S

Pink Lady has it all: distinctive color, intense flavor, a beautiful shape, and a glamorous, campy name evoking the grenadine-laced cocktail of the same name, stirred by Della Street, perhaps, or a distraught blonde in a 1960s Perry Mason mystery.

It is a large, conical apple with a deep pink blush covering green skin. Its cream-colored flesh is dense, and its sweet-tart taste has hints of citrus. Pink Lady is good for both fresh eating and cooking. It holds its shape when cooked, and it stores well.

Originally named Cripps Pink, Pink Lady became the first variety to be sold and marketed under a trademarked name. It was developed by John Cripps at the Department of Agriculture and Food in Western Australia. Lady Williams, an Australian apple from the 1930s, gives Pink Lady its characteristic shade. Golden Delicious supplies its yellow-green base and conical shape.

If the apple has too much of the base coloring, Pink Lady reverts to Cripps Pink—the apple must be two-thirds pink to qualify for the premium name. To heighten pink color, some growers remove leaves from the tops of the trees to admit more light, or place reflective strips on the ground beneath the rows of trees to increase sunlight to fruit on lower branches.

Red Astrachan

ORIGIN		DISCOVERED	RELEASED
Russia		1700s or older	
PARENTAGE		**HARVEST**	**FLAVOR SCALE**
unknown		Early season	T **2** 3 4 S

Red Astrachan (AS-truh-kuhn) is a medium-size red apple with yellow highlights on a thin skin. It is moderately juicy, with a mild, tart flavor that is better for cooking than fresh eating. It is a good early-season choice for pies and applesauce. It does not store well, and its crisp flesh can become mealy soon after it is ripe. Its skin may break if left on the tree for too long. It is one of New England's earliest varieties, ripening by the end of July.

Red Astrachan is a very old apple from Russia, of unknown origin. It migrated westward to Sweden in 1780, England in 1816, arriving in America in the early 1830s, one of four Russian apples (with Alexander, Duchess of Oldenburg, and Tetofsky) received by the Massachusetts Horticultural Society from the London Horticultural Society.

Red Astrachan's popularity peaked around 1900, when it was grown worldwide. It was especially popular for a time in the American South.

Red Delicious | Hawkeye

ORIGIN		DISCOVERED	RELEASED
Peru, Iowa		1870s	1895
PARENTAGE		HARVEST	FLAVOR SCALE
unknown		Late season	T 2 3 4 **S**

Although its popularity appears to have peaked, Red Delicious remains the most widely grown apple in the United States, and it is the most commercially successful apple of all time. It has remarkable consistency in color, a distinctive, conical shape, and it is excellent for shipping and storing. The trees are easy to grow and highly productive.

A solid, striking red, it may be the most reliably monochromatic apple. Lightly aromatic with crisp, cream-colored flesh, it is an all-purpose apple, best eaten fresh, but also good cooked. It is shipped all over the world, recognizable anywhere.

Its consistency is a weakness of Red Delicious as well as a strength. Its predictably sweet flavor lacks character, and it can be cloying or bland. It faces competition from other sweet apples, such as Gala, which has a distinctive pearlike flavor, and a host of other varieties that offer a broader range of flavors and textures.

Discovered on the farm of Jesse Hiatt, the apple that came to be known as Red Delicious was called Hawkeye until 1893. After it won an apple competition that year sponsored by Stark Brothers Nurseries, C. M. Stark is alleged to have bit into one and said, "My that's delicious—and that's the name for it!" Hawkeye was reissued as Red Delicious two years later.

Red Gravenstein

ORIGIN	DISCOVERED	RELEASED
Origin unknown	1800s	
PARENTAGE	**HARVEST**	**FLAVOR SCALE**
A sport of Gravenstein	Early season	T 2 **3** 4 S

Red Gravenstein, a sport variety of Gravenstein, is both redder in color and less tart than its parent. It is a medium-size apple, slightly blunt and conical. Its cream-colored flesh is crisp and juicy, with a nicely balanced, sweet-tart flavor.

Gravenstein, a European apple from the 1600s, has produced several nearly identical red strains over the centuries; the one called Red Gravenstein was first cited in 1873.

A second red Gravenstein is also called Red Gravenstein, but it is better known as Banks. It was discovered in Nova Scotia about 1880.

Redcort | Red Cort, Red Cortland

ORIGIN	DISCOVERED	RELEASED
Marlboro, New York	1983	
PARENTAGE	**HARVEST**	**FLAVOR SCALE**
A sport of Cortland	Midseason	T **2** 3 4 S

Redcort is a sport variety of Cortland, with heavy red streaking over yellow-green skin. It is a large, oblate apple with crisp and juicy white flesh. Its flavor is more tart than sweet, and it is an outstanding all-purpose apple.

Redspy | Double Red Northern Spy, Red Spy

ORIGIN	DISCOVERED	RELEASED
Victor, New York	1895	1923
PARENTAGE	**HARVEST**	**FLAVOR SCALE**
A sport of Northern Spy	Late season	T 2 **3** 4 S

Redspy is a sport variety of Northern Spy, but with a rich ruby color over a green skin rather than its parent's pinkish red. In other respects, it closely resembles Northern Spy, a large apple with spicy, sweet-tart flavor. Its cream-colored flesh is crisp, aromatic, and juicy. It is good for both fresh eating and cooking.

It was discovered on the farm of William S. Greene, and presented at the New York State Agricultural Experiment station by his son, C. E. Greene, in 1910.

Rome Beauty | Rome

ORIGIN	DISCOVERED	RELEASED
Rome, Ohio	1816	1848
PARENTAGE	**HARVEST**	**FLAVOR SCALE**
unknown	Late season	T **2** 3 4 S

Rome Beauty is a medium-to-large round apple with a deep red color and excellent storage qualities. Rome's greenish white flesh is crisp and juicy, with sweet-tart flavor; it has a thick skin. It is good eaten fresh but is particularly prized as a cider apple and for baking, as it holds its shape well.

A tree planted nearly two centuries ago by H. N. Gillet on the banks of the Ohio River produced a shoot from below the graft—the part of the tree that is not supposed to bear fruit. Growers generally trim these unwanted shoots off, but this branch survived to bear beautiful red fruit.

While its popularity has begun to wane in New England in recent years, only one other apple on America's top ten list, McIntosh, discovered around 1800, is older than Rome Beauty.

Royal Gala | Tenroy

ORIGIN	DISCOVERED	RELEASED
New Zealand	1970s	
PARENTAGE	HARVEST	FLAVOR SCALE
A sport of Gala	Midseason	T 2 3 4 **S**

Royal Gala is a red strain of Gala, a New Zealand native that is among the most widely grown apples in the world. Medium in size and conical, Royal Gala has stunning red-orange color deeper than its parent, but shares its sweet, pearlike flavor. It is an all-purpose apple and outstanding for fresh eating.

Royal Gala was named by W. M. McKenzie in honor of Queen Elizabeth II, who was so impressed with Gala given to her during a visit to his orchard that she requested more. She was not the only monarch to travel to the orchard where Royal Gala was discovered: Juliana, queen of the Netherlands, visited in 1971.

Sansa

ORIGIN	DISCOVERED	RELEASED
Japan and New Zealand	1970	1988
PARENTAGE	HARVEST	FLAVOR SCALE
Akane × Gala	Early season	T 2 3 **4** S

Sansa is medium-size, round, and typically red in color, but it can also appear with a deep pink blush on a yellow skin. It is a sweet, juicy apple with crisp, light green flesh. Considered best for fresh eating, it is one of the better early-season apples.

Sansa is the result of an unusual collaboration between researchers in Japan and New Zealand. The apple's parents are Japan's early-season Akane and New Zealand's Gala, which gives Sansa its characteristic sweetness. In 1969, Japanese apple breeder Dr. Yoshio Yoshida sent pollen harvested from Akane blossoms to Dr. Donald McKenzie in

New Zealand, to cross-pollinate with Gala. Gala was not grown in Japan at the time, and Akane was not available in New Zealand.

McKenzie returned seeds from this cross to Yoshida, and the resulting trees were evaluated for nearly 20 years before the variety's 1988 release. Unfortunately, McKenzie did not live to see the result of their joint effort, as he died in a car accident that same year.

Sheep's Nose | Black Gilliflower, Red Gilliflower

ORIGIN	DISCOVERED	RELEASED
Connecticut	1700s	
PARENTAGE	**HARVEST**	**FLAVOR SCALE**
unknown	Midseason	T 2 **3** 4 S

Sheep's Nose is a stunning apple to look at, less good to eat. Its names extols its pronounced conical shape and deep ruby color. Often solid red, it can also have patches of green. An aromatic apple, its dense flesh is lacking in juice, and it becomes drier in storage. Its mild, sweet-tart flavor is good in cooking, especially in applesauce, and it has had a small but steady following. It has endured for more than two centuries, having been reported in New England as early as the Revolutionary War.

A number of other apples have been called Sheep's Nose, and the name has been used as a synonym for Bullock, Egg Top, Lady Finger, Long Red Pearmain, and Yellow Transparent.

Spartan

ORIGIN	DISCOVERED	RELEASED
Summerland, British Columbia	1926	1936
PARENTAGE	**HARVEST**	**FLAVOR SCALE**
McIntosh × unknown	Late season	T 2 3 **4** S

Spartan is a dark, plum-red apple with chewy skin and tender, aromatic white flesh. It has good sweet-tart flesh with hints of strawberry and

spice, and is moderately juicy. It is best as a fresh-eating apple. It keeps well. The trees need heavy thinning, though, or the apples will be too small, and they are susceptible to apple scab.

Spartan was developed by R. C. Palmer at Canada's Federal Agriculture Research Station, now known as the Pacific Agri-food Research Centre. For many years it was described as a cross between McIntosh and Newtown Pippin, but as a result of recent genetic testing, the latter has been ruled out, leaving Spartan's second parent a mystery.

Stark Jumbo

ORIGIN	DISCOVERED	RELEASED
Hood River, Oregon	1958	1966
PARENTAGE	**HARVEST**	**FLAVOR SCALE**
A sport of Spokane Beauty	Late season	T 2 **3** 4 S

Stark Jumbo is a huge, boxy apple, mostly red apple with yellow highlights. It is crisp and juicy, with sweet, tangy flavor. It can easily weigh more than 2 pounds. It is best used in cooking.

Stark Jumbo is a strain of Spokane Beauty, a large apple from Washington State dating to 1859.

Stayman | Stayman Winesap

ORIGIN	DISCOVERED	RELEASED
Leavenworth, Kansas	1866	1875
PARENTAGE	**HARVEST**	**FLAVOR SCALE**
Winesap × unknown	Late season	T 2 **3** 4 S

Stayman is a striped, cherry red apple with prominent lenticels and some russeting. It has tender, juicy, cream-colored flesh. Its flavor is more sweet than tart, with hints of honey, and it is highly aromatic. It resembles its Winesap parent, but tends to grow larger, and its color is not as deep. It is an all-purpose apple that stores well.

Stayman was first grown by Dr. Joseph Stayman. As it requires a long growing season, it is mostly a southern apple, and it is not widely grown in New England.

Sweet Sixteen

ORIGIN	DISCOVERED	RELEASED
Minnesota	1973	1977
PARENTAGE	HARVEST	FLAVOR SCALE
Frostbite × Northern Spy	Midseason	T 2 3 **4** S

Sweet Sixteen is a large, boxy apple, red overlaid on green-yellow skin, with prominent white lenticels. Its yellow flesh is crisp and juicy. It has a sweet, spicy flavor with hints of citrus and vanilla. Its Frostbite parent imparts a complexity to Sweet Sixteen's flavor resembling sugar cane.

Sweet Sixteen was introduced by the Minnesota Agricultural Experiment Station of the University of Minnesota. It has the same parentage as Keepsake. Both varieties were released decades before Frostbite, however, which made its debut as a named apple in 2008.

Williams' Pride

ORIGIN	DISCOVERED	RELEASED
West Lafayette, Indiana	(1975)	1988
PARENTAGE	HARVEST	FLAVOR SCALE
Jonathan, Melba, Mollie's Delicious, and Rome, among others	Early season	T 2 **3** 4 S

Williams' Pride is a medium-size to large, slightly conical, maroon red apple. Its cream-colored flesh is crisp and juicy, with a spicy, sweet-tart flavor. It is an all-purpose apple especially good for fresh eating.

It was developed by the Indiana, New Jersey, and Illinois (PRI) joint apple-breeding program, and named for Edwin B. Williams, long-time head of the disease-resistant apple-breeding program at Purdue University. Its heritage includes Jonathan, Melba, Mollie's Delicious, and Rome.

It is not to be confused with the heirloom apple Williams, discovered in Roxbury, Massachusetts, in the mid-1700s.

Winesap

ORIGIN	DISCOVERED	RELEASED
Moorestown, New Jersey	1700s	
PARENTAGE	**HARVEST**	**FLAVOR SCALE**
unknown	Late season	T 2 3 **4** S

Winesap is small, round, cherry red in color with a chewy skin. It has crisp, light yellow flesh, and is moderately juicy. It has outstanding flavor, more sweet than tart, with hints of cherry. It is an all-purpose apple, and it is especially good for fresh eating and for cider. It stores well. Although some have suggested it has a winelike flavor, it is more likely that it received its name for its deep red color.

Winesap requires a long season, and it is primarily a southern apple. It was widely grown in the 19th century in the South, especially in Virginia, and it remained popular until about 1950. Its decline was hastened by its generally small size and the advent of controlled atmosphere (CA) storage, which made its outstanding storage quality less important.

Its age and origin are unknown, but it was first recorded by Dr. James Mease in 1804, and it is generally thought to have come from New Jersey sometime before 1800.

Ananas Reinette

ORIGIN	DISCOVERED	RELEASED
Netherlands or France	1500s	
PARENTAGE	**HARVEST**	**FLAVOR SCALE**
unknown	Late season	T 2 **3** 4 S

Ananas Reinette (ah-na-nas reh-NET) is a beautiful apple, small, round, slightly oblate, mostly yellow over a green skin, with prominent green or brown lenticels, or pores. Ananas Reinette has crisp, juicy, white flesh, and a sweet-tart flavor with hints of pineapple (ananas is French for "pineapple"). Its flavor intensifies in storage.

It was first recorded in 1821 in Germany, but may have originated in Netherlands or France in the 16th century. Its arrival in America is not documented; it received scant mention in reference works before 1950.

Blondee

ORIGIN	DISCOVERED	RELEASED
Portsmouth, Ohio	1998	
PARENTAGE	**HARVEST**	**FLAVOR SCALE**
A sport of Kidds D-8 Gala	Midseason	T 2 3 **4** S

Blondee is a round, medium-size to large apple with smooth, yellow skin and an occasional red blush. Its crisp flesh is moderately juicy, more sweet than tart, and a little spicy. It is good for fresh eating and in salads, as it browns slowly when sliced. It does not bruise easily, and it stores well.

Discovered on the farm of Tom and Bob McLaughlin in Portsmouth, Ohio, overlooking the Ohio River, Blondee is now a trademarked variety.

Blushing Golden | Blushing Gold

ORIGIN	DISCOVERED	RELEASED
Cobden, Illinois	1959	1968
PARENTAGE	HARVEST	FLAVOR SCALE
Jonathan × Golden Delicious	Late season	T 2 3 **4** S

Blushing Golden is a medium-size to large, conical apple, yellow with a pink-orange blush. Its skin is on the tough side, and its cream-colored flesh is crisp and juicy. Its sweet-tart flavor with hints of honey becomes more complex in storage. It stores well and does not bruise easily. It is a good all-purpose apple.

Blushing Golden was discovered on the farm of Ralph B. Griffith.

Calville Blanc d'Hiver | White Calville

ORIGIN	DISCOVERED	RELEASED
France or Germany	1500s	
PARENTAGE	HARVEST	FLAVOR SCALE
unknown	Late season	T 2 **3** 4 S

Calville Blanc d'Hiver (kal-vil BLANGK dee-vehr) is a medium-size to large, ribbed apple with a yellow-green skin and an occasional pink blush. Its aromatic, cream-colored flesh is spicy, more tart than sweet, and its flavor intensifies in storage. It is high in vitamin C. One of Thomas Jefferson's favorite apples, it is mostly used in cooking and in cider. It stores well.

Its age and origin are unknown, but it was first cited in 1598 France. It was recorded visually at an early date, too: Calville Blancs and the small, round Lady apple appear to be the subjects of Claude Monet's oil painting Still Life with Apples and Grapes from 1880.

Claygate Pearmain

ORIGIN		DISCOVERED	RELEASED
Surrey, England		Early 1800s	
PARENTAGE		**HARVEST**	**FLAVOR SCALE**
unknown		Late season	T 2 **3** 4 S

Claygate Pearmain is a small, round or conical apple with occasional red blush and light russeting on a yellow-green skin. Its cream-colored flesh is aromatic and crisp, but only moderately juicy. A good fresh-eating apple, its nutty flavor is nicely balanced between sweet and tart. It stores well, and the trees are disease-resistant.

Claygate Pearmain won several awards in its early decades, and it was popular in Victorian England. It was discovered growing along a hedge by John Braddick. He also discovered the apple called Braddick's Nonpareil, which was briefly popular in the United States in the early 1800s.

Ginger Gold

ORIGIN		DISCOVERED	RELEASED
Lovingston, Virginia		1969	
PARENTAGE		**HARVEST**	**FLAVOR SCALE**
Golden Delicious × Newtown Pippin (possible)		Early season	T 2 3 **4** S

Ginger Gold is a medium-size to large, round to conical apple with a smooth, green-yellow skin, often with a light pink blush. Its crisp, juicy, white flesh is more sweet than tart. Ginger Gold is good for both cooking and fresh eating, especially in salads, as its flesh browns slowly when sliced. It is an outstanding early-season apple.

It was discovered in the orchard of Clyde and Ginger Harvey in the foothills of Virginia's Blue Ridge Mountains. Clyde Harvey originally wanted to name the apple "Harveylicious," but a marketing consultant persuaded him to use his wife's first name instead. Its parentage is not certain, but it may include both Golden Delicious and Albemarle Pippin.

Golden Delicious | Mullins Yellow Seedling

ORIGIN	DISCOVERED	RELEASED
Clay County, West Virginia	1890	1916
PARENTAGE	HARVEST	FLAVOR SCALE
unknown	Late season	T 2 3 4 **S**

Golden Delicious is one of the most widely planted apples in the world, and parent to a number of other varieties. It is a medium-size to large, conical apple, golden yellow in color with an occasional pink blush and russeting around the stem. Its yellow flesh is crisp, aromatic, and juicy, and it has rich, mellow, sweet flavor, with hints of honey. It is an outstanding apple for fresh eating, and it is also good in cooking, especially in pies, as its flesh holds up well when cooked. It is an excellent keeper.

Although it shares its conical shape and many flavor characteristics with Red Delicious, the two apples are unrelated. Discovered by Anderson H. Mullins near the town of Odessa, West Virginia, and originally called Mullins Yellow Seedling, Golden Delicious was renamed by Stark Brothers Nursery when it was introduced commercially in an effort to replicate the success of the Red Delicious. It may be a seedling of Grimes Golden.

It is West Virginia's official state fruit.

Golden Supreme

ORIGIN		DISCOVERED	RELEASED
West Virginia		Age unknown	
PARENTAGE		HARVEST	FLAVOR SCALE
unknown		Early season	T 2 3 **4** S

Golden Supreme is a medium-size to large, conical apple, yellow with prominent brown lenticels and a pink-orange blush. Its cream-colored flesh is crisp and juicy, and it has a pleasant but mild sweet-tart flavor. It is an all-purpose apple especially good for fresh eating, in cider, and in salads, as its flesh browns slowly. It stores well.

Its age and origin are unclear; while generally credited to Clay County, West Virginia, some accounts say that it is from Idaho.

GoldRush

ORIGIN		DISCOVERED	RELEASED
West Lafayette, Indiana		1973	1993
PARENTAGE		HARVEST	FLAVOR SCALE
Golden Delicious × (Siberian Crab, Winesap, Melrose, Rome Beauty)		Late season	T 2 **3** 4 S

GoldRush is a medium-size to large, round to conical apple, golden yellow with an orange-red blush. It is crisp and juicy, with a complex, spicy, sweet-tart flavor that mellows over time. It is an all-purpose apple especially good for fresh eating, in cider, and in salads, as it is slow to brown. It stores exceptionally well, and its trees are disease resistant.

It was developed by PRI, the joint apple-breeding program of Purdue University, Rutgers University, and the University of Illinois. It was named Illinois's official state fruit in 2008.

Gold Spy | New York 315

ORIGIN	DISCOVERED	RELEASED
Geneva, New York	1979	
PARENTAGE	**HARVEST**	**FLAVOR SCALE**
Golden Delicious × Northern Spy	Late season	T **2** 3 4 S

A large, attractive, yellow apple with an orange blush, it was originally listed as New York 315 in the New York State Fruit Testing Cooperative Association's "Catalog of New and Noteworthy Fruits," and it is sometimes found by that name. Sam and Susan Averill of Averill Farms in Washington Depot, Connecticut, purchased trees of the variety in 1979 from a nursery in New York State, and christened it Gold Spy. "We have quite a few trees that were planted as experimental numbered varieties," says Susan, "some of which were later named and some of which were not, causing us to call them something!"

Its flesh is crisp, and its flavor is tarter than that of Spigold, which has the same parents. Gold Spy is good eaten fresh, but is used more for cooking. It ripens late, after Red Delicious but before Golden Delicious, and it has a long storage life.

Gold Spy was developed at the New York State Agricultural Experiment Station.

Granny Smith

ORIGIN	DISCOVERED	RELEASED
Sydney, Australia	1860s	
PARENTAGE	**HARVEST**	**FLAVOR SCALE**
unknown	Late season	**T** 2 3 4 S

Granny Smith has been the most popular green apple in the world since its arrival in the United States in the 1970s. Medium-size, round, and slightly oblate, it has nearly solid green color with an occasional pink blush. Its white flesh is crisp and juicy, and it has refreshingly tart flavor,

with strong hints of citrus. It is good for both fresh eating and cooking, and it stores exceptionally well.

Maria Ann Smith, who emigrated from England to Australia, discovered the first Granny Smith seedling in a marsh on her property, possibly from the seed of a French Crab. It was first exported to England in the 1930s.

Granny Smith has reached its commercial peak but remains popular around the world. It requires a long growing season, so only a handful of New England orchards have had success with Grannies, but as the climate warms, that number is increasing.

New England-grown Granny Smith apples are apt to have a pink or red blush.

Green Newtown Pippin

ORIGIN		DISCOVERED	RELEASED
Newtown (now Elmhurst), New York		Early 1700s	
PARENTAGE		HARVEST	FLAVOR SCALE
unknown		Late season	T 2 **3** 4 S

Green Newtown Pippin is a medium-size, round, oblate apple, green with occasional russeting around the stem or a pink blush. Its crisp, juicy flesh is pale yellow, and it is aromatic, with sweet, moderately tart flavor. It is an all-purpose apple especially good in cider. It is a good keeper.

Green Newtown Pippin is often confused with Yellow Newtown Pippin. The trees are so similar that it is likely that one is a sport variety of the other, though it is impossible to say which came first. Many early references dropped the color from the name altogether, referring to either apple as simply "Newtown Pippin," further blurring the distinction.

The separate strains were first recorded in 1817, but by then it already had an illustrious history as the first American apple to attract significant attention in Europe. Benjamin Franklin brought grafts to England in the mid- to late-1700s, where the apple was known as Newton Pippin of New York. It could have been either Green Newton Pippin or Yellow Newton Pippin.

The original tree grew in Newtown, Long Island, New York, near a swamp on the farm of Gershom Moore.

Grimes Golden | Grimes, Grimes Golden Pippin

ORIGIN	DISCOVERED	RELEASED
West Virginia	Early 1800s	
PARENTAGE	**HARVEST**	**FLAVOR SCALE**
unknown	Midseason	T 2 **3** 4 S

Grimes Golden is a medium-size round apple, gold to deep yellow in color. Its yellow flesh is crisp, aromatic, and moderately juicy, and its flavor is spicy, more tart than sweet. It is good for fresh eating and in cider.

It may be parent to a more famous apple also from West Virginia, Golden Delicious. There is misinformation circulating about Grimes Golden, specifically that it grew from seeds left by John Chapman ("Johnny Appleseed"). Chapman planted orchards in only two states, Indiana and Ohio.

Grimes Golden is held in high esteem in its native West Virginia, in any case. Wood from the trunk of the original tree (which blew down in a storm in 1905 after bearing fruit for more than a century) was used to make gavels for the West Virginia Agricultural Society. A portion of the trunk is preserved at West Virginia University, and a stone monument marks the site of the original Grimes Golden tree.

Mutsu | Crispin

ORIGIN		DISCOVERED	RELEASED
Mutsu Province, Japan		1930	1948
PARENTAGE		**HARVEST**	**FLAVOR SCALE**
Golden Delicious × Indo		Late season	T 2 3 **4** S

Mutsu is a large, slightly conical apple ranging in color from green to yellow, often with an orange blush. Its crisp, pale yellow flesh is aromatic, sweeter than tart, and juicy. It is more tart than either of its parents, Golden Delicious and Indo, a Japanese variety from the 1930s. Mutsu is an all-purpose apple, especially good in salads as its flesh browns slowly, and in pies. In addition to its flavor and size, Mutsu holds its shape when cooked. It stores extremely well.

Originally named for a province in Japan, it was renamed Crispin in England in 1968.

Porter | Summer Pearmain, Yellow Summer Pearmain

ORIGIN		DISCOVERED	RELEASED
Sherburne, Massachusetts		1800	
PARENTAGE		**HARVEST**	**FLAVOR SCALE**
unknown		Early season	T 2 3 **4** S

Porter is a medium-size, round, greenish yellow apple with a crimson-orange blush. Its cream-colored flesh is tender, aromatic, and juicy. Its flavor is sweeter than tart. Porter is a good all-purpose apple, and it retains its shape and flavor when cooked.

It was discovered by Rev. Samuel Porter, but was primarily a local apple until 1850, when its popularity spread to Boston and it began to be grown in other parts of the country. In his 1922 book *Cyclopedia of Hardy Fruits*, U. P. Hedrick wrote, "A generation ago Porter took rank as one of the best of all yellow fall apples. If the fruits be judged by quality, the variety would still rank as one of the best of its season, but the apples are too tender in flesh to ship, the season of ripening is long and variable, and the crop drops badly.

"Porter must remain, then, an apple for the connoisseur, who will delight in its crisp, tender, juicy, perfumed flesh, richly flavored and sufficiently acidulous to make it one of the most refreshing of all apples."

Pristine

ORIGIN	DISCOVERED	RELEASED
West Lafayette, Indiana	1975	1994
PARENTAGE	**HARVEST**	**FLAVOR SCALE**
Camuzat × Co-Op 10	Early season	T **2** 3 4 S

Pristine is a medium-size, round apple with lemon yellow skin and a pink blush. A crisp, juicy apple with pale yellow flesh, its sweet-tart flavor has hints of citrus. Pristine is unusually crisp for an early-season apple, and it stores well compared to many early varieties. It is one of the earliest apples to ripen, in mid-August.

Pristine was developed by PRI, the joint apple-breeding program of Purdue University, Rutgers University, and the University of Illinois, with pollen from a numbered seedling crossed with Camuzat, a little-known apple from Spain. Its ancestry includes Golden Delicious, McIntosh, Red Delicious, and Rome Beauty.

Pumpkin Sweet | Pound Sweet, Rhode Island Sweet, Vermont Sweet

ORIGIN	DISCOVERED	RELEASED
Manchester, Connecticut	1830s	
PARENTAGE	**HARVEST**	**FLAVOR SCALE**
unknown	Late season	T 2 3 4 **S**

Pumpkin Sweet is a large, boxy, ribbed apple, yellow to green with a golden brown blush and patches of russeting, particularly near the stem.

Its crisp, cream-colored flesh is sweet but lacks strong flavor. It is best as a cooking apple, and it stores well.

Pumpkin Sweet is one of several varieties discovered by S. Lyman of Manchester, Connecticut. It was mostly a local apple for half a century, but eventually spread throughout New England and New York State, and for a time it was popular in the South. It was generally marketed under the name Pound Sweet.

Rhode Island Greening

ORIGIN		DISCOVERED	RELEASED
Green's End, Rhode Island		1600s	
PARENTAGE		**HARVEST**	**FLAVOR SCALE**
unknown		Late season	**T/2** 3 4 S

Rhode Island Greening is one of America's oldest apples, the most well known and successful to have originated in Rhode Island, where it is the official state fruit. It is a large, round or boxy apple, usually solid green in color with an occasional pink blush. Its crisp white flesh is moderately juicy, with delicately tart flavor. It is an outstanding cooking apple as well as good for fresh eating. It bruises easily, and is highly susceptible to apple scab, but it keeps well.

Rhode Island Greening is more than green in color; it was discovered by a Mr. Green, an innkeeper in Green's End near Newport. So many scions were removed from the original tree that it died, according to U. P. Hedrick, who also asserts that the apple was not discovered until 1748.

Rhode Island Greening became well known in the 1700s, and it enjoyed a lengthy reign as the nation's most popular green apple, so much so that Andrew J. Downing, in his 1845 book Fruits and Fruit Trees of America, wrote, "The Rhode Island Greening is such a universal favorite, and is so generally known, that it seems almost superfluous to give a description of it."

At the beginning of the 20th century it was still one of the top three varieties grown in the Northeast, with two other New England apples, Baldwin and Northern Spy, and it was widely grown until the 1930s.

Shamrock

ORIGIN	DISCOVERED	RELEASED
Summerland, British Columbia	1992	
PARENTAGE	**HARVEST**	**FLAVOR SCALE**
Spur McIntosh × Spur Golden Delicious	Midseason	T **2/3** 4 S

Due to its similar size, color, and flavor, Shamrock has been promoted as an East Coast alternative to the horticulturally challenging Rhode Island Greening or the slower-growing Granny Smith. But it shares many characteristics with its McIntosh parent. Medium-size to large, it is round, and solid green with occasional pink blush. It has tender, cream-colored flesh. Its flavor is tart when first picked, with a sweet finish hinting of honey and butterscotch. Like many apples, its flavor improves in storage, becoming progressively sweeter, spicier, and juicier for several weeks. It is an all-purpose apple, especially good for fresh eating. Its storage life is short.

It was developed at Canada's Pacific Agri-Food Research Centre in British Columbia.

Shizuka

ORIGIN	DISCOVERED	RELEASED
Aomori, Japan	1969	1986
PARENTAGE	**HARVEST**	**FLAVOR SCALE**
Golden Delicious × Indo	Late season	T 2 3 **4** S

A large, round to conical, green-yellow apple with a red-orange blush, Shizuka has the same parentage as Mutsu, but its flavor and texture are very different. Shizuka's distinctive light crisp flesh is similar to that of

Honeycrisp and Jonagold. It is sweeter than Mutsu. It is outstanding eaten fresh or in a salad, as it is slow to brown once cut. It stores well.

Shizuka was developed by Tsuneo Murakami in Aomori prefecture. It resembles Jonagold, too, in its lack of commercial success in the United States. Perhaps both apples need snappier names.

Silken

ORIGIN	DISCOVERED	RELEASED
Summerland, British Columbia	1982	1998
PARENTAGE	HARVEST	FLAVOR SCALE
Honeygold × Sunrise	Early season	T 2 3 4 **S**

Silken is a medium-size, conical apple, pale yellow with an occasional pink blush or russeting around the stem. Its tender, cream-colored flesh is aromatic and juicy, and it has mild, sweet flavor. It is best eaten fresh, and it has a short storage life.

It was developed by W. D. Lane and R. A. MacDonald at Canada's Pacific Agri-Food Research Centre.

Tolman Sweet | Tallman's Sweet

ORIGIN	DISCOVERED	RELEASED
Massachusetts	1700s	
PARENTAGE	HARVEST	FLAVOR SCALE
unknown	Late season	T **2** 3 4 S

Tolman Sweet is a medium-size, pale yellow apple with occasional red or green blush and russeting. It sometimes has a distinctive line running from top to bottom. Its white flesh is crisp and moderately juicy, and its flavor is unusual, sweet and pearlike. It is an all-purpose apple, especially good in cooking and in cider. Its trees are exceptionally hardy, making it a good choice in northern climes, but the fruit bruises easily.

Tolman Sweet may be a cross of Sweet Greening and Old Russet discovered in Dorchester, Massachusetts, but its origin is not clear. It was first cited in 1822, and it remained popular well into the 20th century.

Winter Banana

ORIGIN	DISCOVERED	RELEASED
Cass County, Indiana	1876	1890
PARENTAGE	**HARVEST**	**FLAVOR SCALE**
unknown	Late season	T 2 3 **4** S

Winter Banana is a large, round or boxy apple with pale yellow skin and a light red blush. Its white flesh is crispy, aromatic, and moderately juicy, and it is considered better for fresh eating than cooking due to its mild, sweet flavor. It is also good in cider. Most people do not detect any banana flavor; the apple's name likely comes from its color. It bruises easily, but stores reasonably well.

It was discovered on the farm of David Flory in Adamsboro, Indiana. While still grown in parts of the Midwest, its main use in New England is to pollinate other varieties.

Yellow Bellflower | Lady Washington, Lincoln Pippin

ORIGIN	DISCOVERED	RELEASED
Crosswicks, New Jersey	Late 1700s	
PARENTAGE	**HARVEST**	**FLAVOR SCALE**
unknown	Midseason	T **2** 3 4 S

Yellow Bellflower is a medium-size to large, conical, lemon yellow apple with a light red-orange blush. Its cream-colored flesh is crisp, juicy, and aromatic, and its tart flavor mellows in storage. It is best used in cider and for cooking, especially in pies. It bruises easily and does not store well.

One of the oldest heirloom apples from New Jersey, it was not much grown in New England until after 1850. Its name may come from the fact that it hangs like a bell from the tree.

Yellow Newtown Pippin | Albermarle Pippin

ORIGIN		DISCOVERED		RELEASED
Newtown (now Elmhurst), New York		Early 1700s		
PARENTAGE		**HARVEST**		**FLAVOR SCALE**
unknown		Late season		T 2 **3** 4 S

Yellow Newtown Pippin is medium-size to large, and predominantly green with yellow blush and red streaks. Its skin is thick but its flesh is crisp and moderately juicy, and it has a pleasant, mildly citrus flavor. It stores exceptionally well.

Yellow Newtown Pippin has had greater name recognition and commercial success as Albemarle Pippin. The apple found its way south from Long Island with Dr. Thomas Walker, an officer under General Edward Braddock during the French-Indian War. After Braddock's forces were defeated trying to capture Fort Duquesne in 1755, Walker returned to his Castle Hill plantation in Virginia's Albemarle County carrying scions from a Yellow Newtown tree. When the trees grafted with these bore fruit the apple was renamed Albemarle Pippin. Thomas Jefferson wrote that he had grafts of Albemarle Pippin in 1773, and they were planted at his Monticello plantation in 1778. Albemarle Pippin was a major export to England for nearly a century beginning in the mid-1700s.

Yellow Newtown Pippin is often confused with Green Newtown Pippin. The trees are so similar that it is believed that one is a "sport" of the other, though it is impossible to know which is the original. Many early accounts further blur the distinction by dropping the color from the name, referring to one as simply "Newtown Pippin."

The two varieties are distinguished by their size, color, and flavor.

Yellow Transparent

ORIGIN		DISCOVERED	RELEASED
Russia		Age unknown	
PARENTAGE		HARVEST	FLAVOR SCALE
unknown		Early season	T 2 3 **4** S

The origin of Yellow Transparent's name is evident when sunlight strikes a ripe apple on the tree, seeming to illuminate the fruit as it passes through. It is a medium-size, round apple, mostly yellow in color. Moderately crisp and juicy, Yellow Transparent has white flesh and a light, sweet flavor with just a hint of tartness. It is ripe by August, and should be used soon after it is harvested, as it does not store well.

Yellow Transparent is of undetermined age but has Russian roots. It was brought to America by Dr. T. H. Hoskins, of Newport, Vermont, in 1870.

Ashmead's Kernel

ORIGIN		DISCOVERED	RELEASED
Gloucester, England		1700s	
PARENTAGE		**HARVEST**	**FLAVOR SCALE**
unknown		Midseason	T 2 **3** 4 S

Ashmead's Kernel has the richest flavor of almost any apple. It is a medium-size to small, roundish apple, with heavy russeting and an orange blush over a bumpy, copper-colored skin. Its cream-colored flesh is crisp and juicy, and its sweet-tart flavor is complex, with hints of vanilla, orange, pear, nutmeg, lemon, and tea. "Its initial Madeira-like mellowness of flavor overlies a deeper honeyed nuttiness, crisply sweet not sugar sweet," wrote the late food writer Philip Morton Shand. "Surely no apple of greater distinction or more perfect balance can ever have been raised anywhere on earth."

Its outstanding flavor gets even better in storage, and it stores well. An all-purpose apple, it is especially good eaten fresh and in cider.

William Ashmead discovered it in his garden, growing from a chance seedling. The term kernel is synonymous with "pippin" or "seed."

Belle de Boskoop | Reinette Monstrueuse, Reinette von Montfort

ORIGIN		DISCOVERED	RELEASED
Boskoop, Holland		1856	
PARENTAGE		**HARVEST**	**FLAVOR SCALE**
unknown		Late season	T **2** 3 4 S

Belle de Boskoop is a medium-size to large, round, boxy apple with russeting around the stem and in a netting pattern over much of its distinctive orange-red skin. Its crisp, light green flesh is sweet-tart with hints of lemon. It is an aromatic apple, moderately juicy, and it remains firm in cooking. It keeps well, and its flavor becomes sweeter in storage.

Belle de Boskoop was discovered by K. J. W. Ottolander in his nursery in Boskoop, near Gouda. It was introduced in North America in Canada around 1880.

D'Arcy Spice

ORIGIN	DISCOVERED	RELEASED
Tolleshunt D'Arcy, Essex, England	1785	1848
unknown	Late season	T 2 **3** 4 S

D'Arcy Spice is a round, medium-size to small apple, with patches of russet and red-orange over chewy yellow-green skin. Its cream-colored flesh is aromatic, tender to crisp, with nicely balanced flavor between tart and sweet. Its light, spicy flavor has hints of nutmeg. Its flavor becomes sweeter and more complex in storage.

Discovered growing in a garden in 1785, it is an old apple from southeast England. It was introduced by nurseryman John Harris in 1848 with the name Baddow Pippin.

Golden Russet

ORIGIN	DISCOVERED	RELEASED
Western New York	1800s	
PARENTAGE	**HARVEST**	**FLAVOR SCALE**
unknown	Late season	T 2 3 4 **S**

Golden Russet is a medium-size to small, round apple with light brown russeting over green skin. Its cream-colored flesh is crisp and juicy, and its flavor sweet, with a hint of honey. An all-purpose apple, its exceptional sweetness makes it a favorite with cider-makers, and it is especially good for fresh eating. It stores well.

Its origin is in western New York, and it is distinct from several varieties similar in name or appearance, including English Golden Russet,

Hunt Russet, and an apple from Massachusetts known as Golden Russet. It may be a seedling of English Golden Russet.

In 1905, S. A. Beach noted that Golden Russet's popularity was waning, suffering the fate of many russets: "In recent years the season of good red winter apples has been extended by means of cold storage with the result that long keeping russet apples are less profitable."

Hudson's Golden Gem

ORIGIN	DISCOVERED	RELEASED
Tangent, Oregon	1931	
PARENTAGE	**HARVEST**	**FLAVOR SCALE**
unknown	Late season	T 2 3 4 **S**

Hudson's Golden Gem is a medium-size, conical apple with light russeting over a green-gold skin. Its cream-colored flesh is crisp and juicy, and its superior sweet flavor has hints of nut and pear. An all-purpose apple, it is outstanding eaten fresh and used in cider. It stores well.

Hudson's Golden Gem was discovered as a seedling along a fence at the Hudson Nursery in Tangent, Oregon. With its elongated form, bronze russeting, and evocative flavor, it was originally marketed as a pear.

Knobbed Russet | Knobby Russet

ORIGIN	DISCOVERED	RELEASED
Sussex, England	1819	
PARENTAGE	**HARVEST**	**FLAVOR SCALE**
unknown	Late season	T 2 3 **4** S

Knobbed Russet is so ugly it must be good. It is a small, misshapen apple, and its gnarly, russeted skin is covered with warts and welts. That it has survived for so long attests to its superior flavor. Like the frog prince of fairy tales, Knobbed Russet's character is magically transformed when eaten. Its dense, cream-colored flesh has little juice, but its flavor is complex, sweet and nutty. It is best eaten fresh or used in cider. It stores well.

If its odd appearance is not enough of a handicap, Knobbed Russet trees can be difficult to grow. It had nearly died out by the 1940s, when its virtues were rediscovered during England's national fruit trials.

Orleans Reinette | Winter Ribston

ORIGIN	DISCOVERED	RELEASED
France	1700s	
PARENTAGE	**HARVEST**	**FLAVOR SCALE**
unknown	Late season	T 2 3 **4** S

Orleans Reinette (or-leenz reh-NET) is an unusually striking apple, medium-size to large, round, oblate, with random patches of russet and bronze blush on a rosy red skin. Its cream-colored flesh is crisp and juicy, and it has a complex sweet, nutty flavor, with hints of orange. Its flavor matches its appearance. The late food writer and pomologist Edward Bunyan considered Orleans Reinette "the best tasting apple in the world."

The first reference to Orleans Reinette is from 1776. It is one of a number of "reinette" varieties (*reinette* is a French word of indeterminate meaning), most of which are very old, dating back to at least the 1700s.

Pitmaston Pineapple | Reinette d'Ananas, Pineapple Pippin

ORIGIN	DISCOVERED	RELEASED
Pitmaston, England	1780s	1845
PARENTAGE	**HARVEST**	**FLAVOR SCALE**
unknown	Midseason	T 2 **3** 4 S

Pitmaston Pineapple is a small, round or conical apple with solid russet covering bronze skin. It has crisp, cream-colored flesh without much

Russeted Apples

juice, but a sweet, nutty flavor with a hint of honey, and a pineapple taste that gives the variety its name. Its small size diminishes its value as a cooking apple, but it is outstanding for fresh eating and good in cider.

Pitmaston Pineapple was first grown by a Mr. White about 1785, possibly from the seed of a Golden Pippin. It was presented to the London Horticultural Society in 1845 by a Mr. Williams of Pitmaston.

Pomme Grise | French Russet, Gray Apple

ORIGIN		DISCOVERED	RELEASED
Canada		Early 1800s	
PARENTAGE		HARVEST	FLAVOR SCALE
unknown		Late season	T 2 3 **4** S

Pomme Grise has many similarities with Pitmaston Pineapple: it is a small, round apple with chewy, green-yellow skin coated with brown russet. It tends to grow a little larger than Pitmaston, though, and its skin is coarser. Its pale yellow flesh is firm, crisp, and aromatic, with a unique nutty, sweet and spicy flavor, making it especially good for cider.

Pomme Grise was grown around Montreal before making its way south to New York's St. Lawrence Valley, and eventually New England. It may be related or identical to a 16th-century French apple called Reinette Grise.

Roxbury Russet | Boston Russet, Leather Coat

ORIGIN		DISCOVERED	RELEASED
Roxbury, Massachusetts		1635	
PARENTAGE		HARVEST	FLAVOR SCALE
unknown		Late season	T 2 3 **4** S

Roxbury Russet is generally considered America's oldest cultivated apple variety. It is medium-size, round, with coarse russeting covering chewy yellow skin, and sometimes-prominent white or yellow lenticels.

Its yellow-green flesh is coarse, crisp and juicy. Its intense, sweet, spicy flavor is as good for fresh eating as it is for cider. Like most russets, it stores well.

It migrated from Massachusetts to Connecticut by 1649, and then on to Marietta, Ohio, in 1796, with Rufus and Israel Putnam. In addition to New England, in the 1800s it was widely grown in New York and Michigan, and was known in the marketplace simply as "Russet" or "Rox." It has had many names over the years, including Belpre Russet, Hewe's Russet, Marietta Russet, Putnam's Russet, Shippen's Russet, Sylvan Russet, and Warner Russet.

Zabergäu Reinette

ORIGIN	DISCOVERED	RELEASED
Württemberg, Germany	1885	
PARENTAGE	**HARVEST**	**FLAVOR SCALE**
unknown	Midseason	T 2 3 **4** S

Zabergäu Reinette (ZAH-bur-gow reh-NET) is a medium-size to large, copper-colored apple with light russeting covering yellow skin. Its crisp, cream-colored flesh is moderately juicy, and its spicy, sweet, and nutty flavor intensifies in storage. It is good for fresh eating and in cooking, especially in pies, and it keeps well.

Zabergäu Reinette was first grown on the Zaber River in southwestern Germany. It began to be widely distributed in 1926.

Restricted Apples

Ambrosia

ORIGIN		DISCOVERED	RELEASED
Similkameen Valley, British Columbia		1980	1993
PARENTAGE		HARVEST	FLAVOR SCALE
Jonagold × unknown?		Late season	T 2 3 **4** S

Ambrosia is a medium-size to large, conical apple with an almost fluorescent pink or orange-red blush over yellow skin. Its aromatic, juicy, cream-colored flesh is mostly sweet, lightly tart, with hints of pear. It is good for fresh eating and in cider and salads, as its flesh browns slowly when sliced. Ambrosia does not store particularly well.

Wilfrid and Sally Mennell discovered this chance seedling near a row of Jonagold trees in their orchard. Golden Delicious and Red Delicious had previously been planted on the site.

Envy | Scilate

ORIGIN		DISCOVERED	RELEASED
New Zealand		1985	2012
PARENTAGE		HARVEST	FLAVOR SCALE
Braeburn × Royal Gala		Late season	T 2 3 4 **S**

Envy is a medium-size to large, conical apple, mostly red-orange over yellow skin, sometimes with prominent white lenticels. Its crispy, cream-colored flesh is moderately juicy. Its flavor is cotton-candy sweet, with hints of honey and vanilla. An all-purpose apple, its flesh is slow to brown, making it good in salads.

The first cross of Envy was made by farmer Allan White. It has the same Braeburn and Royal Gala parents as Jazz, and both apples were developed in New Zealand in the 1980s. Envy is harvested in June and July in New Zealand, and in late October where it is grown in Washington State and in Canada. It is not available in New England's supermarkets until midwinter.

Jazz

ORIGIN	DISCOVERED	RELEASED
New Zealand	1980s	2000
PARENTAGE	**HARVEST**	**FLAVOR SCALE**
Braeburn × Royal Gala	Late season	T 2 **3** 4 S

Jazz appears to have everything needed for commercial success: it is colorful to look at and sweet to eat, yet tough enough for the demands of storing and shipping. It comes with a short, snappy, easy-to-remember name, even if it has nothing to do with apples. It is a medium-size to large, conical apple, red to maroon with green and orange-gold patches. Its yellow flesh is dense and juicy, sweet with hints of pear. It stores extremely well.

Like Envy, Jazz is a cross between New Zealand's two biggest commercial stars of the last century, Braeburn (1952) and Royal Gala (1934), but with very different results.

Junami | Diwa, Milwa

ORIGIN	DISCOVERED	RELEASED
Jegenstorf, Switzerland	1985	2012
PARENTAGE	**HARVEST**	**FLAVOR SCALE**
(Idared × Maigold) × Elstar	Late season	T **2** 3 4 S

Junami is a round, oblate apple, mostly red over yellow. Its flesh is dense and juicy, and it has sweet-tart flavor with hints of citrus. Its flavor continues to develop in storage, and it stores well.

Milwa, the tree on which the apple is grown, is trademarked, as are its apples, which are sold under the brand name Junami. It was developed by Markus Kellerhals and Alfred Aeppli for the Swiss Federal Research Station. It is rarely available in New England before January.

Restricted Apples

Kiku

ORIGIN	DISCOVERED	RELEASED
Northern Italy	1990	2009
PARENTAGE	**HARVEST**	**FLAVOR SCALE**
A sport of Fuji	Late season	T 2 3 4 **S**

Kiku is a medium-size to large, round apple, mostly red with a few yellow streaks and highlights. Its light crisp, juicy flesh is similar in texture to Jonagold or Honeycrisp, and it is very sweet, with a hint of citrus. It keeps well.

A sport variety of Fuji, Kiku is redder and sweeter than its parent. It was discovered by South Tyrolean apple breeder Luis Braun during a visit to Japan.

Lady Alice

ORIGIN	DISCOVERED	RELEASED
Gleed, Washington	1979	2009
PARENTAGE	**HARVEST**	**FLAVOR SCALE**
Parents unknown	Late season	T 2 3 **4** S

Lady Alice is a large, round apple with heavy orange-red and pink striping over yellow skin. It has dense, juicy flesh. Its sweet flavor, with a hint of citrus, develops further in storage. Lady Alice is an all-purpose apple, especially good in salads, as its flesh browns slowly when cut, and baking, as it holds its shape when cooked.

Lady Alice is a chance seedling discovered by Don Emmons in his orchard. While he was cultivating around his trees, a disc from his plow hit the base of a Red Delicious. The damaged tree sent out a new shoot that became Lady Alice.

It is sold exclusively by the Rainier Fruit Company and named for Alice Zirkle, who cofounded the company with her husband Lester. It usually is not available in New England until February.

Rubens | Civni

ORIGIN	DISCOVERED	RELEASED
Ferrara, Italy	1985	2003
PARENTAGE	**HARVEST**	**FLAVOR SCALE**
Gala × Elstar	Late season	T 2 3 **4** S

Rubens is a medium-size to large, conical apple, mostly red with yellow streaking. It has thin skin and light crisp, juicy, cream-colored flesh with a green tinge. Its flavor is sweet with light tartness, and it is good for all purposes. It stores well.

It was developed by the Consorzio Italiano Vivaisti, a growers' consortium.

It is a different variety from an apple from the Netherlands named Rubens developed in 1954 from a cross of Cox Orange Pippin and Reinette Etoilée.

RubyFrost | New York #2

ORIGIN	DISCOVERED	RELEASED
Geneva, New York	1992	2013
PARENTAGE	**HARVEST**	**FLAVOR SCALE**
Braeburn × Autumn Crisp	Late season	T 2 **3** 4 S

RubyFrost is a medium-size to large, round, oblate apple with rich red color. Its flesh is juicy, and it has balanced, sweet-tart flavor. It has a high vitamin C content, probably from its Braeburn parent. It is good for both fresh eating and cooking. It stores well.

RubyFrost made a modest debut at New York farmers' markets in 2013, and its production is scheduled to increase in 2014. It is not predicted to be in grocery stores in significant quantities until 2015. It was developed by Susan K. Brown at the New York State Agricultural Experiment Station.

SnapDragon | New York #1

ORIGIN		DISCOVERED	RELEASED
Geneva, New York		1998	2013
PARENTAGE		**HARVEST**	**FLAVOR SCALE**
Honeycrisp × numbered seedling		Midseason	T 2 3 **4** S

SnapDragon is a medium-size, conical red apple with occasional yellow highlights. Its distinctive, light crisp texture is similar to that of its Honeycrisp parent. Its flavor is sweet and spicy, making it especially good for fresh eating. It stores well.

SnapDragon, like RubyFrost, made its debut at New York farmers' markets in 2013, with production scheduled to increase in 2014. It is not predicted to appear in grocery stores in significant quantities until 2015. It was developed by Susan K. Brown at the New York State Agricultural Experiment Station.

Sonya | Nevson

ORIGIN		DISCOVERED	RELEASED
New Zealand		2000	2002
PARENTAGE		**HARVEST**	**FLAVOR SCALE**
Gala × Red Delicious		Year-round	T 2 3 4 **S**

Sonya is a medium-size to large, conical apple like its Gala and Red Delicious parents, but it has reddish orange color over yellow skin. Its crisp flesh is aromatic and sweet. It is good for all purposes, especially fresh eating. It stores well.

Named for the daughter of the grower who developed it, it was introduced as Sonya in 2002.

SweeTango

ORIGIN	DISCOVERED	RELEASED
Minnesota	1988	2009
PARENTAGE	**HARVEST**	**FLAVOR SCALE**
Honeycrisp × Zestar!	Early season	T 2 **3** 4 S

SweeTango is a medium-size to large, round, oblate apple, mostly red with yellow highlights and prominent white lenticels. Its crisp flesh is juicy, and it has a balanced sweet-tart flavor. It is good for both fresh eating and cooking. It does not store well.

One of the most celebrated apples to enter the marketplace in recent years, it attracted lots of publicity when released by its management company, optimistically named Next Best Thing. So far, though, SweeTango has not lived up to the hype. Granted, much of the media coverage was about the controversy surrounding trademarked apples rather than SweeTango itself. But to date, not only can it not be grown in New England, few of the apples have reached its grocery stores.

It was developed by the University of Minnesota.

Tentation | Delbush

ORIGIN	DISCOVERED	RELEASED
France	1979	1990
PARENTAGE	**HARVEST**	**FLAVOR SCALE**
Golden Delicious × Blushing Golden (Grifer)	Year-round	T 2 **3** 4 S

Tentation is medium-size to large, conical apple, golden yellow with a pink-orange blush. It has crisp, juicy, cream-colored flesh, and a sweet-tart flavor with hints of citrus, banana, and pear. It is an all-purpose apple, good for both fresh eating and cooking. It stores well, but bruises easily.

It was developed by the Delbard nursery in France.

Cider Apples

Chestnut Crab Apple

ORIGIN	DISCOVERED	RELEASED
Minnesota	1946	1949
PARENTAGE	**HARVEST**	**FLAVOR SCALE**
Malinda × unknown	Midseason	T 2 3 **4** S

Chestnut Crab Apple is small, round, with a rosy red blush and some russeting over a yellow base. Unlike many crab apples, its dense, cream-white flesh is mostly sweet and nutty, with hints of vanilla and citrus. In addition to cider, it is good for fresh eating. It does not store well.

It was developed at the University of Minnesota.

Dabinett

ORIGIN	DISCOVERED	RELEASED
Somerset, England	Early 1900s	
PARENTAGE	**HARVEST**	**FLAVOR SCALE**
unknown	Late season	—

Dabinett is a small, round apple with strawberry red highlights on yellow-green skin. Its juice is bittersweet and astringent.

Discovered growing in a hedge by William Dabinett, it is believed to be a seedling of Chisel Jersey, a 19th-century cider apple, also from Somerset.

Egremont Russet

ORIGIN	DISCOVERED	RELEASED
Somerset, England	Mid-1800s	
PARENTAGE	**HARVEST**	**FLAVOR SCALE**
unknown	Late season	T 2 **3** 4 S

Egremont Russet is a medium-size, round apple, with russet over golden skin. It has cream-colored flesh and a balanced sweet-tart, nutty flavor (late food writer Morton Shand likened it to crushed ferns). It is an all-purpose apple and good for fresh eating, but in New England today it is grown primarily for use in fresh and hard cider.

It was first recorded in 1872 by nurseryman J. Scott, but may have originated earlier on the estate of Lord Egremont in Sussex.

Harrison

ORIGIN	DISCOVERED	RELEASED
Essex County, New Jersey	Early 1800s	
PARENTAGE	HARVEST	FLAVOR SCALE
unknown	Late season	T **2** 3 4 S

Harrison is medium-size, round to conical, and its rich, yellow skin often has prominent brown or black lenticels. Its yellow flesh is crisp but dry. Harrison juice makes an exceptionally dark, rich cider. It stores well.

It was named for the family that discovered it, and it was grown throughout the eastern United States until the early 1900s. Like Egremont Russet, it can be eaten fresh or used in cooking, but it is now known chiefly for its properties in cider.

Harry Masters Jersey | Port Wine

ORIGIN	DISCOVERED	RELEASED
Somerset, England	1800s	
PARENTAGE	HARVEST	FLAVOR SCALE
unknown	Late season	—

Harry Masters Jersey is a medium-size, round apple, red with some russeting. It adds a medium to full bittersweet quality to hard cider. It does not store well.

It is believed to have been discovered by Harry Masters in Yarlington Village, South Somerset.

Cider Apples

Hewes Crab Apple | Virginia Crab Apple

ORIGIN		DISCOVERED	RELEASED
Virginia		Early 1700s	
PARENTAGE		**HARVEST**	**FLAVOR SCALE**
unknown		Midseason	—

Hewes Crab Apple is a small, round apple with red striping over yellow-green skin and white lenticels. Its crisp yellow flesh adds dryness and a complex, sweet-tart flavor to cider, usually mixed with other varieties.

An old apple from Virginia, it was a favorite of Thomas Jefferson.

King David

ORIGIN		DISCOVERED	RELEASED
Washington County, Arkansas		1893	1902
PARENTAGE		**HARVEST**	**FLAVOR SCALE**
Jonathan × Arkansas Black		Late season	T 2 **3** 4 S

King David is a medium-size, round, dark red apple. It has crisp, juicy, yellow flesh and a spicy flavor that is outstanding in fresh and hard cider. All purpose, good for fresh eating, it was discovered along a fencerow.

Kingston Black

ORIGIN		DISCOVERED	RELEASED
Somerset, England		Late 1800s	
PARENTAGE		**HARVEST**	**FLAVOR SCALE**
unknown		Midseason	—

Kingston Black is small, dark red over yellow skin, with some russeting. It is aromatic and has a distinctive, bitter, sweet-tart flavor that is outstanding in hard cider. The trees are susceptible to several diseases and can be difficult to grow. It is one of several 19th-century cider apples from Somerset that remain popular today.

Redfield

ORIGIN	DISCOVERED	RELEASED
Geneva, New York	1924	1938
PARENTAGE	HARVEST	FLAVOR SCALE
Wolf River × Niedzwetzkyana Red Crab	Late season	T 2 3 4 S

Redfield is a medium-size, round to conical apple, cherry red with prominent white lenticels. Its dry, tender, cream-colored flesh is tinged red near the skin. Its flavor is too tart for fresh eating, but it is used in cooking in addition to cider. It does not store well.

It was developed at the New York State Experiment Station, and for many years was advertised as an ornamental tree.

Reine de Pomme

ORIGIN	DISCOVERED	RELEASED
Northern France	1800s	
PARENTAGE	HARVEST	FLAVOR SCALE
unknown	Midseason	—

Reine de Pomme is a medium-size to small, round apple, red with yellow stripes and some russeting. Its juice is sweet and astringent, and it adds a bittersweet quality to hard cider.

A native of France, it was introduced in England in 1903.

Tremlett's Bitter

ORIGIN	DISCOVERED	RELEASED
Devon, England	Late 1800s	
PARENTAGE	HARVEST	FLAVOR SCALE
unknown	Midseason	—

Tremlett's Bitter is a medium-size, round to conical apple, mostly red with yellow highlights and a little russet around the stem. Its crisp white

Cider Apples

flesh is tart, and its juice is sweet and astringent, contributing a full bittersweet quality to hard cider.

Wickson | Wickson Crab

ORIGIN		DISCOVERED	RELEASED
Humboldt County, California		1944	
PARENTAGE		**HARVEST**	**FLAVOR SCALE**
Cross of unnamed crab apples		Late season	T 2 3 **4** S

Wickson is a small, round, cherry red apple. It has juicy, tender flesh, and its potent combination of sweet and tart flavors makes it an outstanding addition to fresh and hard cider. Its trees are hardy and disease resistant.

It was developed by pomologist Albert Etter, who named it for his friend, Edward J. Wickson, the long-time dean of the College of Agriculture at the University of California and author of several books, including *The California Fruits and How to Grow Them* (1909).

Yarlington Mill

ORIGIN		DISCOVERED	RELEASED
Somerset, England		Early 1900s	
PARENTAGE		**HARVEST**	**FLAVOR SCALE**
unknown		Late season	—

Yarlington Mill is a medium-size to small, round apple with red streaking over yellow skin. It has crisp, white flesh and flavor that lends a medium bittersweet quality to hard cider.

The original tree was found growing out of a wall near a water wheel in Yarlington or North Cadbury by a Mr. Bartlett. After being transplanted to a nearby garden, it was probably grown by Harry Masters.

5

RARE

NEW ENGLAND
Apples

It would be virtually impossible to catalog all of the named cultivated apples that have been discovered in New England over the past 400 years, and of little practical use, since the vast majority of them are now extremely rare or extinct (or presumed so). The 200-plus apples listed here have been chosen because of their unusual histories or because they are still known to be grown somewhere in New England. A few non-native varieties are included because they enjoyed a period of commercial success in the region.

Apples come and apples go. Across the globe, new apple varieties have been continually under development for centuries—it is estimated that there are more than 8,000 varieties grown somewhere on Earth today. Literally thousands have been discovered in New England since the Mayflower landed at Plymouth Rock in 1620, including America's first named variety, the Roxbury Russet, in 1635. A vast number of these early apples were still in existence a century ago. Speaking to a group of growers in 1900, pomologist S. T. March of the University of Massachusetts in Amherst said, "I suppose we have between one and two thousand named varieties of apple that are of some importance. Many of them are valuable in certain localities and not in others. It is a fact that almost any variety of large size and good color may become popular in a locality."

While many of these old and obscure varieties may now be extinct, one or more trees may yet grow unrecognized somewhere in the countless small and home orchards throughout New England's rural countryside, in suburban backyards, or even along city streets, waiting to be rediscovered. More than 100 pre-1900 varieties are preserved at Tower Hill Botanic Garden in Boylston, Massachusetts, and many of them are photographed here.

Roxbury Russet is still grown today, and is now making a mild comeback for its excellence in fresh and hard cider. But most of New England's earliest varieties have not passed the test of time, just as many of the new varieties in today's produce aisles will likely fade from view eventually, their commercial success limited by some horticultural, shipping, or storage flaw, or because the fruit simply lacks distinction.

The trees may bear small or unreliable crops, be susceptible to pests, or otherwise be challenging to grow. The variety may produce fruit only every other year. The apples may be small or misshapen, have tough skin, or keep poorly in storage. Some apples that were known for such traits as hardiness or excellence in storage, lost value as a result of climate change and advances in rootstocks, refrigeration, and controlled atmosphere storage.

An apple can fail to capture the public's imagination for a variety of reasons. Its flavor may be perfectly passable, but not distinctive enough to create lasting demand. Russeted or dull, yellow-green apples are rejected by customers desiring shiny red, gold, or green fruit. Some apples suffer from poor branding, with easily forgettable, unimaginative names. Such words as *sweet*, *pearmain*, and *pippin* appear in so many apple names before 1850 they become hard to distinguish, and they are usually paired with the obscure name of the landowner who discovered the apple, or the town in which the orchard was located.

Until the mid-19th century, virtually every New England household kept a small orchard of apples for their sweetness, versatility, year-round availability, and especially for making cider, fresh and hard. It was not necessary for an apple to be good eaten fresh as long as it excelled in cooking or juice, and cider was the nation's drink, fresh and hard, young and old. So when a Mr. Abbott tasted a highly edible, sweet apple from a tree he found growing by a stone wall near his New Hampshire orchard, it was noteworthy and worth propagating. Abbott might graft a few onto some of his less desirable trees. Perhaps he would give or sell a few to his friends and neighbors. A cousin might take some scions to his home in Connecticut or Maine.

The apple might be renamed in its new locale, remaining popular for decades and attracting many loyal followers. But sooner or later it would be supplanted by newer, better varieties, or it would be lost or forgotten when the original trees died or the farm was sold off.

Yet many of these rare apples survive and continue to excel for certain uses, and their trees may thrive in some locales. In addition to their wide range of flavors, colors, and textures, and their nutritional value, these apples add to our genetic diversity; some may yet become parents to future varieties with better qualities.

The orchard, the apple tree, its blossom, and its fruit are dynamic, living works of art, complex and ever changing. Each apple is living history, a replica from the original tree on which it was discovered, sometimes hundreds of years ago.

Locating one of these rare gems today can be as satisfying as an apple's crunch.

Abbott's Sweet originated in New Hampshire and was first cited in 1845. Conical in shape, yellow with red patches or stripes and prominent lenticels, its white flesh is crisp and juicy, its flavor pleasantly sweet.

◄ **American Beauty** (Beauty of America, Sterling Beauty) was probably discovered in the 1850s by O. V. Hills in Sterling, Massachusetts, now the site of Sunny Crest Orchards. American Beauty is a large apple, sweet and aromatic with slightly chewy flesh. It has dark red streaks or blush over yellow-green skin, with some russeting. Its dense, cream-colored flesh is coarse and juicy, and it has a complex, spicy flavor with a hint of honey.

◄ **American Golden Pippin** was discovered in the late 1800s, most likely in Maryland. It was valued because the trees were cold hardy and the apples were excellent keepers. Its skin is olive green with a red wash, and a little russeting. The dense, grainy, cream-colored flesh is not very juicy, and the flavor is mild, with a hint of tartness. It is used primarily for cooking or for cider.

Arctic was a chance seedling in a garden near Cape Vincent, New York, around 1862, according to S. A. Beach. It was introduced by O. K. Gerrish of Lakeville, Massachusetts, after Gerrish bought the tree from John Esseltyne in 1887. A hardy apple, Arctic is similar to Baldwin in appearance, but with a more oblate shape and a lighter, brighter red skin. Its mild flavor is lightly tart. After taking propagating wood from it, Gerrish destroyed the tree to prevent theft of scions.

Aunt Hannah was discovered on the farm of Deacon Francis Peabody in Middleton, Massachusetts, and dates back to at least the early 1800s. Aunt Hannah is a small, straw-colored apple with some russeting and a good flavor resembling that of Newtown Pippin.

Averill (Wolf's Den) is from Pomfret, Connecticut, cited in 1845. It is a large, conical apple with greenish skin with yellow striping and a red blush. Its white flesh is crisp and juicy, with a mildly sweet-tart flavor.

Bailey Golden (Bailey's Golden Sweet, Bailey's Golden Winter) originated in the orchard of Paul Bailey, in Sidney, Maine, before 1850. It is a large, oblate, yellow apple with some russet. A late-season apple, its coarse white flesh is sweet.

Baker, of Richfield, Connecticut, dates back to the Revolutionary War, writes Beach. A large red apple similar to Baldwin in shape, flavor, and color, Baker is milder and paler.

Baker Sweet is an old variety discovered near New London, Connecticut, and it was once much grown in parts of New England. First cited in the 1840s, it is a large, yellow, late-season apple with a sweet taste. It does not store well.

Barrett is from Kensington, Connecticut, pre-1840. It is a large, conical apple, yellow with red stripes. Its crisp yellow flesh is juicy, and its flavor is mildly spicy.

Bars originated in Greenwich, Rhode Island, pre-1840. It is a large, early-season apple, mostly red with some russet over a yellow base. It has crisp, juicy, white flesh and mild, sweet flavor.

Belle et Bonne (Golden Ball, Tenor Hills) is a native of Connecticut dating back to at least the early 1800s. Belle et Bonne has large yellow fruit. A late-season apple that stores well, its flavor was too mild to make it a commercial success, although it was "much esteemed" in the Hartford area in the late 1800s, according to Thomas.

◀ **Benoni** originated in Dedham, Massachusetts, in the early 1800s, and was once cultivated widely throughout the United States. An early-season apple, its smooth skin is a beautiful wine red, or orange-yellow, with red stripes, and its yellow flesh is crisp, sweet, and juicy. Benoni's popularity waned due to the smallness of its fruit, and its poor, biennial bearing habit.

Benton Red (Pennock) was discovered in Benton, Maine, before 1800, although most accounts ascribe Pennock to Delaware County, Pennsylvania. Benton Red is an all-purpose apple good for fresh eating, cooking, drying, and cider, and it stores well.

Bethel originated in Bethel, Vermont, in the mid-1800s. Bethel resembles the pearmain group of apples with its pearlike shape, quality, texture, and rich, dark red color. Bethel has good flavor and its trees are hardy. But it bruises easily, making it unsuitable for shipping.

Blakely is from Pawlet, Vermont, sometime before 1850. It is large and oblate, with yellow skin and patches of red. Its flesh is crisp and juicy, and its flavor mildly sweet-tart.

Boardman is a late-season apple from Maine in the 1800s, light yellow in color with splashes of red. It has crisp, juicy flesh and a tart flavor.

Bottle Greening is a chance seedling discovered in an orchard on the Vermont–New York border and first cited in the 1860s. Bottle Greening was considered excellent for culinary use, but its tender skin bruised easily, and it did not store well. One story behind its name is that workmen found a hollow in the original tree to be a convenient place to stash "the bottle."

Boxford originated on the farm of Peter Towne in Boxford, Massachusetts, circa 1825. It has red stripes on a yellow skin, "the flesh is tender, and the flavor excellent," wrote Kenrick.

Brigg's Auburn is a midseason apple from Auburn, Maine, first cited in 1845. It is large, oblate, with yellow skin and a pink blush. Its white flesh has a pleasing sweet-tart flavor.

Buck Meadow was discovered in Norwich, Connecticut, prior to 1845. Slightly conical in shape, it is yellow with patches or streaks of red. Its yellow flesh is juicy, with a spicy flavor.

Burr's Winter Sweet is from Elisha Burr of Hingham, Massachusetts, pre-1850. Burr's Winter Sweet is a sweet, early-season apple, yellow with red splashes or stripes. It has crisp, juicy, yellow flesh.

Cake is from Connecticut, dating back to the early 1800s. It is oblate, juicy, and yellow with a pink or red blush.

Carter (Royal Pippin) was discovered by Nathanial Carter of Leominster, Massachusetts, before 1850. A round, late-season apple, it has yellow skin with patches of red. Its tender flesh is mildly sweet.

Cathead, a large, conical, ribbed English apple dating to the 1600s, is pale green, with crisp, juicy flesh and mildly sweet-tart flavor. It is a midseason apple used mostly for cooking.

Champlain (Haverstraw Pippin, Large Golden Pippin, Nyack, Sour Bough, Summer Pippin, Tart Bough) was mostly cultivated in New England. The first account of it was in an 1853 edition of *New England Farmer*, but its origin is unknown. Its name may be linked to Vermont's Lake Champlain, although it was equally well known as Nyack or Summer Pippin. Champlain is of good quality, and the trees are hardy, long-lived, and productive. Its greenish yellow skin limited Champlain's consumer appeal.

◀ **Chandler** was discovered on the farm of Francis Richardson in Chelmsford, Massachusetts, and it was introduced by General Samuel Chandler of Lexington in the early 1800s, although it has also been identified as having originated in Connecticut. A large apple, Chandler is pinkish red with yellow patches or striping. Its flesh is crisp and juicy, and it has good flavor, sweet with a little tartness.

Cogswell was discovered on the farm of Fred Brewster in Griswold, Connecticut, in the early 1800s. It is a large, aromatic apple good for fresh eating, with red stripes over yellow skin.

Colton (Early Colton) originated in Rowe, Massachusetts, about 1840. It is an early-season, greenish yellow apple with unexceptional flavor or color, although for a time it was popular in the Midwest.

Cooper is an old variety of unknown origin, introduced from Connecticut to Ohio by Israel and Rufus Putnam in 1796. It is a late-season apple, light yellow with red striping, mostly sweet.

◀ **Crow Egg** was discovered by Abijah Fisher of Dedham, Massachusetts, and it was first cited in 1832. It is a medium-size apple with red stripes over a yellowish skin and an oval shape that gave it its name. Its dense white flesh has outstanding sweet-tart flavor, and it stores well. It is distinct from Crow's Egg, another name for Sheep's Nose, in some southern states.

Danvers Sweet (Danvers Winter Sweet, Espes Sweet) was discovered on the Derby farm in Danvers, Massachusetts, in the 1700s. It is juicy, sweet, and has tender yellow-green flesh. Although included in the American Pomological Society's first list of recommended varieties for its sweet flavor and storage qualities, Danvers Sweet fell into disfavor by the beginning of the 20th century, in part because of its dull green to bright yellow skin.

▶ **Deacon Jones** is from Pennsylvania in the late 1800s. A large, bulky apple, tall and conical in shape, it is mostly red in color with a touch of green and some russeting. Its flesh is crisp and juicy, and its flavor is sweet with a light tang.

Dudley (Dudley's Winter, North Star) is a seedling of Duchess of Oldenburg, discovered by J. W. Dudley, of Castle Hill, Aroostook County, Maine, and first described in 1891. It is a large, yellow-green apple covered with red streaks. Its cream-colored flesh is crisp, juicy, and tart at first, mellowing in storage. Dudley's main virtue is the hardiness of its trees, making it briefly popular in northern New England.

Dumelow (Dumelow's Crab, Wellington) was introduced in England in 1820. Large, and conical or irregular, Dumelow is mostly yellow with some red striping. Mildly sweet, it does not store well, and it is best used as a cooking apple.

▶ **Dyer** (Pomme Royale, Woodstock) was discovered in Cranston, Rhode Island, in the 1700s. A large, round apple with greenish yellow skin and some russeting, it sometimes has a pink or brownish blush. Its yellow flesh has a medium crisp texture and a lemony, sweet-tart flavor. It does not ripen evenly, though, requiring multiple pickings from late August to October.

▶ **Early Joe**, like Melon and Northern Spy, grew from seeds collected in the Salisbury, Connecticut, orchard of Heman Chapin after Chapin moved to East Bloomfield, New York. It was introduced in the early 1840s. It is a small, early-season apple with red stripes. It has excellent flavor, but much of its fruit is misshapen or too small.

◀ **Early Strawberry** (Red Juneating, American Red Juneating) is believed to have originated in New York State around 1800. A bright red, early-season apple with occasional yellow streaking, it is good for both fresh eating and cooking. Its juicy, cream-colored flesh is lightly tart and spicy, and it stores well. But the trees are biennial bearers and the apples are often small and misshapen.

Ellis is from Connecticut, pre-1850. It is small, round, yellow-green with a brown blush. Its flesh is crisp and juicy, and it stores well.

Epsy, from Vermont, was cited in the 1840s for its conical shape and deep red color. Its white flesh is richly sweet.

Esten is from Rhode Island, pre-1850. Large, ribbed and oblate, it has prominent lenticels and red and green patches over a yellow skin. Its tender white flesh has mild, sweet-tart flavor.

Eustis (Ben Apple) is from South Reading, Massachusetts, pre-1850. Eustis has red stripes and patches on a yellow skin. An aromatic apple with crisp, yellow flesh, its flavor is mildly tart.

Excel originated in Sharon, Connecticut, before 1850. Large and oblate, it features splashes of red over a yellow skin. Its flesh is crisp, yellow, and juicy, and it has a sweet-tart flavor.

Fairbanks was discovered in Winthrop, Maine, before 1850. Oblate or conical in shape, it is a midseason apple, yellow with red stripes and some russeting. Its yellow flesh is crisp, and it has a spicy flavor.

◀ **Fallawater** is a Pennsylvania native from the early 1800s, once grown in New England. It is a large, round apple, with dull green color and red highlights. Its mild flavor is unremarkable and, while its flesh is crisp, Fallawater has tough, chewy skin.

▶ **Fall Harvey** was discovered in the 1830s in Essex County, Massachusetts. A late-season apple with yellow skin and a red blush, Fall Harvey has broad ribs. It is a hardy tree able to withstand northern New England winters, but its flavor is bland.

Fall Jenneting was first recorded in Connecticut in the early 1800s. Once esteemed for the vigor of its trees, Fall Jenneting's green-yellow fruit bruises easily. It does not ship well or keep well in storage.

Fall Orange was discovered in Holden, Massachusetts, first described in the 1840s. A medium-size to large apple with yellow-green skin and a red blush, it has crisp, juicy, white flesh, with tart flavor. It is considered best for cooking.

▶ **Fall Pippin** is a large yellow late-season apple that was especially valued for cooking. One of America's oldest apples, it was grown in New England in the 1700s, but its origins are unclear. It is aromatic, with crisp, juicy, cream-colored flesh and outstanding sweet-tart flavor, and it stores well. The trees are susceptible to scab, however, and the fruit ripens unevenly.

Fay's Russet originated in Bennington, Vermont, before 1850. A small, conical apple, it is pale yellow with a red blush or streaks. Its white flesh is spicy and sweet-tart.

Felch is a large, conical apple from Limerick, Maine, pre-1850. It is greenish yellow with patches of dull red, with crisp flesh and mild sweet-tart flavor. A late-season apple, it stores well.

Fisk's Seedling was discovered in Keene, New Hampshire, prior to 1845. It is a late-season apple, oblate, mostly red in color with some yellow. Its tender flesh is greenish white, and it has a sweet, spicy flavor.

Flat Sweeting (Hornet Sweeting) came from Plymouth County, Massachusetts, pre-1825. As its two names indicate, this yellow apple has a flat shape, and its sweet juice makes it a favorite of hornets.

Foundling (River Apple) is from Groton, Massachusetts, with references dating to the 1840s. Foundling is an early-season apple, yellow-green with red stripes, with crisp, white, juicy flesh and a pleasant sweet-tart flavor.

French's Sweet was discovered in Braintree, Massachusetts, cited in 1854. A green, aromatic apple that turned yellow when fully ripe, French's Sweet was described by F. R. Elliott as the "richest baking apple I know."

Garden Royal was discovered in Sudbury, Massachusetts, in the early 1800s. It has a deep yellow skin striped with orange-red and dark crimson. Its flesh is light crisp and aromatic, with sweet-tart flavor. Garden Royal apples were too small and its season too short for commercial value.

Giles is from Wallingford, Connecticut, described in 1854. Giles is a juicy, dark red, late-season apple.

◀ **Gilpin** (Carhouse) was discovered in Virginia in the early 1800s and grown for a time in New England. Small to medium-size and conical, it is mostly red with a hint of orange over a yellow base. A good keeper, its flavor is mild and sweet, its skin heavy, and its flesh a little dry.

Golden Ball (Golden Apple) is an aromatic apple once popular in Maine, especially in the Portland area, from the mid-1800s. It is generally said to have been discovered in Connecticut, and it may be synonymous with Belle et Bonne. It is ribbed and yellow in appearance, juicy and sweet in taste.

▶ **Golden Harvey** (Brandy) is a medium-size to small russeted apple on yellow skin, with occasional streaks of red. A late-season apple, it originated in Herefordshire, England, in the 1600s, and was named after Dr. Gabriel Harvey. Its flesh is juicy and sweet, but very dense. It is especially valued in cider, and it stores well.

▶ **Golden Pippin** is of unknown origin, but it was first referenced in the 1860s and was grown in parts of New England and New York during the late 19th century. A medium-size to large, ribbed apple, yellow-green in color with a pink blush, its flavor is pearlike, sweet and bland.

Golden Pippin, a second apple by the same name, came from Adams, Massachusetts, and was cited in 1869. Yellow-green with a pink blush, its large fruit is slightly conical. It has a sweet-tart flavor, most useful for cooking.

Golden Russet of Massachusetts is distinct from either English Golden Russet or Gold Russet from western New York. Originating in Essex County sometime before 1840, it is a small russeted apple with rich sweet flavor.

Golden Sweet (Golden Sweeting, Orange Sweeting, Yellow Sweeting) is generally traced to Connecticut in the early 1800s. At one point it was held "in high estimation at Providence, where it is brought in sloops from Hartford, Connecticut," wrote Kenrick. Golden Sweet was known for its rich, sweet flavor. Its commercial deficiencies included its clear yellow or dull orange color.

Green Sweet (Green Sweeting, Honey Sweeting) was widely grown in northeastern Massachusetts in the early 1800s, but its origins are uncertain. Green Sweet was considered excellent for both fresh eating and cooking, and it was well regarded for its storage qualities. Its commercial potential was limited due to its dull, green-yellowish skin and small fruit size.

Haralson was developed in 1913 at the University of Minnesota's fruit breeding farm in Excelsior, and it was introduced in 1922. A mostly red, late-season apple, it has crisp, juicy, white flesh, and its mildly tart flavor is especially good in baking and in cider making. It stores well. It is a cross between Malinda and Wealthy.

Hartford Sweeting (Champ Sweeting, Spencer Sweeting) was discovered on Spencer Farm near Hartford, Connecticut, before 1830, and introduced by Dr. E. W. Bull. A large, sweet, juicy red apple, it is an excellent keeper. But "the tree grows slow, and pendulous," wrote Kenrick.

Haskell Sweet (Sassafras Sweet Cole) is a Massachusetts native from the farm of Deacon Haskell of Ipswich, first cited in 1840. It is a sweet apple with green-yellow skin, good mostly for cooking. It does not ripen evenly, requiring multiple pickings from mid-September on.

Hawley was discovered on the farm of Matthew Hawley in New Canaan, Connecticut, around 1750, from seeds Hawley obtained from Milford, Connecticut. A large yellow apple good for fresh eating, the trees are poor bearers and susceptible to several diseases.

Hazen was developed by J. Erwin Loard of Pompanoosuc, Vermont, who, according to Beach, said that it was produced "by crossing some fine cultivated variety, record of name now lost, upon an unnamed seedling red winter apple." The date is unknown. It is a large, yellow-green apple with mild, sweet flavor.

Highland Beauty is a seedling of Lady introduced at the Massachusetts Horticultural Society in 1881. Its skin is smooth yellow, with blushes of bright red. Its cream-colored flesh is crisp and juicy, its flavor mildly tart.

Highlander is from Sudbury, Vermont, circa 1840. It has green skin with red patches or stripes. Its white flesh is juicy, and it has a mild, spicy flavor.

▶ **Hightop Sweet** (High Top Sweeting, Summer Sweet, Sweet June) originated in Plymouth, Massachusetts, in the 1600s. Its medium-size fruit has smooth greenish yellow skin with occasional red blush. Its yellow flesh is dry, and its flavor sweet. It was used mostly for baking and drying. Among the earliest of apples, it ripens in late June to July in most areas.

Hill's Favorite is from Leominster, Massachusetts, circa 1840. A roundish, midseason apple, it has yellow skin with patches of red, and prominent white lenticels. Its dense, yellow flesh is juicy and aromatic, with mild, sweet-tart flavor.

Holmes was discovered by J. Holmes of Kingston, Massachusetts, before 1825. Holmes is a late-season apple used mostly in cider.

Hooker was introduced by Judge E. B. Strong of Windsor, Connecticut, first cited in 1845. It is a large, greenish yellow apple with dark red stripes. Its flesh is greenish white and juicy, and it has a pleasing sweet-tart flavor.

Howe's Russet was discovered in Shrewsbury, Massachusetts, before 1850. It closely resembles, and may be a seedling of, Roxbury Russet. Large and oblate, it has heavy russeting on a greenish, copper skin. Its yellow flesh is dense, and it has a strong spicy flavor.

Hunt Russet (Golden Russet, New England Russet, Russet Pearmain) is an old variety dating back to the late 1600s. It was named for the owner of the farm near Concord, Massachusetts, where it was discovered. It has a gold, russeted skin with patches of red. Its flavor, while good, is less distinctive than most russets, but it is an excellent keeper. Its popularity was limited due to its rough skin.

▶ **Huntsman** is a midwestern apple, discovered in Missouri and first cited in 1872. It is a medium-size, round green apple with a red blush. Its flesh is dense and on the dry side, and it has a tough skin but good flavor with a mildly citrus taste.

Hurlbut (Hurlbut Stripe) was discovered in Winchester, Connecticut, in the early 1800s, on the farm of General Leonard Hurlbut. It is medium-size, oblate, and yellow with red streaks or patches. Its crisp white flesh is juicy, with sweet-tart flavor too mild to distinguish itself.

Jabez Sweet is from Middletown, Connecticut, prior to 1850. Jabez Sweet is pale green to dull red in color. It is a sweet, late-season apple.

Jacobs Sweet (Jacobs Winter Sweet), named for Charles Sumner Jacobs of Medford, Massachusetts, dates back to about 1860. Jacobs Sweet is a large, green or yellow apple with a bright blush. It is considered especially good for baking, but it bruises or cracks easily, it stores poorly, and its trees are susceptible to apple scab.

◀ **Jefferis** (Jefferies) is a Pennsylvania apple from 1848, yellow with red blush and prominent lenticels. Its white flesh is tender and moderately juicy. It has outstanding sweet-tart flavor, but ripens unevenly and grows too small for commercial success.

Jewett's Best originated on the farm of S. W. Jewett in Weybridge, Vermont, before 1850. It is large, oblate, and has patches of deep red on green skin. Its cream-colored flesh is crisp and juicy, with mildly sweet-tart flavor.

Johnson was discovered in Brookfield, Connecticut, pre-1850. A round, early-season apple with heavy red patches or striping, its flesh is crisp, sweet, and juicy, but it does not keep well.

John's Sweet is from Lyndsborough, New Hampshire, pre-1850. It is pale yellow with splashes of red. Its flesh is crisp and juicy; Downing described its sweet flavor as "peculiar."

Kenrick (Kenrick's Red Autumn) was discovered in Newton, Massachusetts, around 1820, in the orchard of writer and nurseryman William Kenrick's father, John. It is a juicy, sweet-tart apple with splashes of red on a green skin.

Ketchum's Favorite came from Sudbury, Vermont, before 1850. Medium in size and irregularly shaped, it has pale yellow skin with a pink blush and prominent red lenticels. Its white flesh has outstanding, though mild, flavor.

Kilham Hill is from the farm of Dr. Daniel Kilham in Wenham, Massachusetts, before 1850. It is a large, round yellow apple with red-striped skin. It has good flavor, but tends to become dry and mealy in storage.

Ladies' Sweeting was discovered near Newburgh, New York, and dates back to the early 1800s. One early reviewer called it "the finest winter sweet apple yet known or cultivated in this country." It is a medium-size, conical apple with dull yellow skin and patches or streaks of red; it is juicy and sweet.

Lane's Sweet is from Hingham, Massachusetts, cited in the 1840s. It is a late-season, oblate apple, yellow with a pink blush. Its aromatic, cream-colored flesh is dense but juicy, and its flavor sweet.

▶ **Late Strawberry** was discovered in Aurora, New York, in the 1840s. It is a pale yellow color, striped or splashed red. It is a good fresh-eating apple, with a strong strawberry flavor that gives the variety its name.

Ledge Sweet was introduced by a Mrs. Haven of Portsmouth, New Hampshire, in 1852, although there are references to the apple as early as the 1840s. It is a large, yellow-green apple with reddish russeting, sweet and juicy.

Leicester Sweet was discovered in Leicester, Massachusetts, prior to 1850. A large oblate apple, greenish yellow to dull red, it is good for both fresh eating and cooking.

Leland Spice (Leland Pippin) is from Sherburne, Massachusetts, pre-1850. It is roundish, and mostly red over yellow. Its cream-colored flesh is aromatic and juicy. A tart apple best used in cooking, it is a poor keeper.

Lincoln is from Hallowell, Maine, dating back to at least 1800. It is a yellow apple with a red blush, with good flavor, but it does not store well.

Lincoln Pippin was discovered by Reuben Lincoln in Connecticut, and first cited in 1881. A good all-purpose, medium-size to large yellow apple, it is considered to have good flavor, and is juicy and aromatic.

Lobo was discovered in Canada in 1898. It is a midseason, round-to-conical, red McIntosh strain. Its tender white flesh is tinged pink, and it has many of McIntosh's characteristics, including its juiciness and sweet-tart flavor with hints of strawberry.

Lodi was developed by the New York State Agricultural Experiment Station, and it was introduced in 1924. It is a yellow, early-season apple with tart flavor used best for cooking. A cross between Montgomery and Yellow Transparent, it enjoyed its greatest popularity in New England in the 1960s and '70s. It does not store well.

Long Stem of Connecticut dates to around 1850. Two apples discovered in New England share the same name. It is oblate, yellow, and sweet.

Long Stem of Massachusetts was discovered in East Bridgewater, also around 1850. Its physical description resembles that of the Connecticut apple of the same name: pale yellow and oblate. Its white, juicy flesh is aromatic with a mild flavor, good for both fresh eating and cooking.

Loring Sweeting is from E. Loring of Plympton, Massachusetts, pre-1850. A late-season apple, it is greenish yellow with red highlights, crisp, juicy, and sweet. It is considered especially good for baking.

Lovett's Sweet is from Beverly, Massachusetts, dating to the 1840s. It is a yellow apple with yellow flesh, moderately juicy and sweet.

Lyman's Large Summer is one of several varieties credited to a Mr. Lyman of Manchester, Connecticut, and it was recorded as early as 1845. A large, early-season apple, it is round and pale yellow, with crisp, yellow flesh. Its mildly tart flavor is considered outstanding.

Lyman's Pumpkin Sweet is a large, yellow, late-season apple introduced by Mr. Lyman of Manchester, Connecticut. Sweet and juicy, it is considered especially good for baking.

▶ **Lyscom** (Osgood's Favorite) is from Southborough, Massachusetts, in the early 1800s. It is a large, red-striped apple over green skin. Its flavor is mild but nicely balanced, its flesh crisp.

Mackay Sweeting was discovered by John Mackay in Weston, Massachusetts, about 1825. It is a beautiful apple "the color of bright straw," with a sweet flavor and a touch of tartness, and a good keeper.

Macomber originated in Guilford, Maine, pre-1850. Oblate with yellow skin and red stripes, it has white, lightly tart flesh.

Magnolia is from Bolton, Massachusetts, referenced in the 1840s. Oblate to conical in shape, it is yellow with red stripes and highlights. Its white flesh is juicy and aromatic, with a spicy flavor.

Magog was discovered by William Warren in Newport, Vermont, about 1870. Magog is considered especially good for cooking. The trees are hardy, making it popular for a time in northern New England, but it does not store well. U. P. Hedrick, in his 1922 *Cyclopedia of Hardy Fruits*, wrote that Magog "has been on probation for nearly a half century, not good enough to recommend and too good to condemn."

◄ **Malinda** originated in Orange County, Vermont; it was being planted in Minnesota as early as 1860. It is medium-size, conical, yellow with a pink-orange blush and some russeting. The flesh is crisp, juicy, and sweet, pleasant but undistinguished. Like Magog, Malinda was valued more for the hardiness of its trees than the flavor of its fruit.

Manomet (Horseblock Apple) was discovered near Plymouth, Massachusetts, and named by John Washburn of Plymouth. It was described in 1854. It is a sweet, juicy, early-season apple with a deep yellow skin with a red blush.

Mansfield Russet was introduced by Dr. Joseph Mansfield of Groton, Massachusetts, in the 1840s. Small and conical, its russeted skin is the color of cinnamon. Its dense flesh, while not very juicy, is aromatic and has a sweet, spicy flavor.

◄ **Margil** (Neverfail) is an old French apple dating back to at least 1750 that came to America via England. It is a small, conical apple with streaks of red, orange, and brown, and slight russeting. Its aromatic yellow flesh is juicy and it has outstanding flavor, sweet and complex, with a touch of tartness. It stores well.

Marquis was discovered by the Honorable O. Fiske of Worcester, Massachusetts, circa 1825. Red in color, it is a juicy apple and a good keeper.

Marston's Red Winter is from Nathan Horton of Greenland, New Hampshire, dating back to the mid-1700s. It is slightly conical and features red stripes on a yellow skin. Its cream-colored flesh is juicy, and its sweet-tart flavor improves in storage.

Meach was introduced by J. M. Ketchum of Brandon, Vermont, before 1850. It is a large apple, slightly conical, with red highlights and prominent brown lenticels over a yellow-green skin. Its cream-colored flesh is juicy and aromatic, its flavor mildly sweet-tart.

► **McLellan** (Martin) was discovered in Woodstock, Connecticut, around 1780. A beautiful rich red apple flecked with yellow, McLellan is aromatic, juicy, and sweet, with a mild, pleasant flavor. Although its skin can be tough, McLellan bruises easily, and it sometimes stays green, lacking flavor.

Melvin Sweet (Melvill Sweet) is a late-season apple from Concord, Massachusetts, pre-1850. It is yellow-green with red stripes, juicy and sugary sweet.

Methodist came from Connecticut, with references dating from the 1840s. It is a medium-size, green, slightly conical apple with red highlights. Its white flesh has mild, sweet-tart flavor.

Mexico originated in Canterbury, Connecticut, before 1845. The round fruit is red, with occasional touches of yellow. Its juicy white flesh has traces of red, and it has outstanding flavor.

Milden (Milding) was discovered in Alton, New Hampshire, around 1865. Milden is a bright red apple over a pale yellow skin, with a pleasing, sweet-tart flavor. Perhaps the yellow skin accounted for its eventual loss of favor, or more likely the fact that the trees yielded large crops only every other year.

Minister was discovered on the farm of David Saunders in Rowley, Massachusetts, and introduced by Rev. Dr. Spring of Newburyport, and Robert Manning of Salem, Massachusetts. It was first cited in 1838. Conical and ribbed, with red stripes on a pale green-yellow skin, it has cream-colored flesh and tart flavor. Manning called it "one of the finest fruits New England has ever produced."

Moore Sweet was discovered in the 1840s by J. B. Moore of Concord, Massachusetts. Dull red in color and an excellent keeper, Beach considered it just "acceptable" for culinary use.

Moore's Greening originated in Kensington, Connecticut, prior to 1850. Large, conical, it is yellow-green with a red blush. Its juicy white flesh has a lively, spicy flavor.

Morrison's Red is native to Medfield, Massachusetts, and referenced in the 1840s. It is conical, pale yellow with red stripes. Its flesh is crisp, with mild, "peculiar" flavor, according to Downing.

Moses Wood is from Winthrop, Maine, in the early 1800s. It is an early-season apple, yellow with red stripes, with juicy white flesh and mild sweet-tart flavor. It does not keep well.

◀ **Mother** (Queen Anne) was discovered in Bolton, Massachusetts, before 1845. It was a standard in many old orchards, valued for its beautiful red color with yellow patches, and its crisp, rich, sweet-tart flesh. Its flavor has been compared to the better-known Esopus Spitzenburg, but it is not considered as good, falling short in flavor and storage qualities.

Munson Sweet (Meachem Sweet, Northern Sweet, Orange Sweet, Rag Apple) is said to have originated in Massachusetts in the early 1700s, and was first described in the 1840s. Munson is pale yellow with a pink blush, with juicy, sweet, cream-colored flesh. It is on the dry side, especially in storage. Still, it enjoyed a period of popularity in New York and New England in the late 1800s.

Murphy was discovered by David Murphy of Salem, Massachusetts, before 1840. It resembles Blue Pearmain in its mild flavor and appearance, with light red skin offset by patches of deeper red, and a bluish bloom.

New England Sweeting (Molasses Apple) was first cited in 1817; it is a yellow-green, late-season apple, oblate in shape. Its flesh is crisp, its flavor sweet.

▶ **Newtown Spitzenburg** originated in Newtown (now Elmhurst), Long Island, New York; it was first cited in 1817. Often confused with two other varieties, Vandevere and Esopus Spitzenburg, it is crisp, aromatic, with outstanding flavor, mildly tart mingled with sweet. It bears unreliably, is not considered attractive due to its dull red color, and it is too small to be marketable.

Nodhead (Jewett Red) originated at Hollis, New Hampshire, in the early 1800s, and can still be found in parts of central Maine. It is a late-season apple of the Blue Pearmain type, dark red with a blue bloom. Its sweet-tart flavor is nicely balanced.

▶ **Nonpareil** is a tart, late-season apple of unknown parentage dating back to France in the 1600s. It is small and round or oblate, with yellow-green skin and an orange blush, and occasional russeting. It is especially good in cider.

Northern Sweet was discovered in Chittendon County, Vermont, in the late 1700s, and it was cultivated mostly in the Champlain Valley. It is a yellow apple with a red blush, with juicy white flesh and sweet flavor.

▶ **Northfield Beauty** originated in Northfield, Vermont, in the 1800s. It is an early-season apple with a boxy shape, medium-size to large, with red streaks over a yellow-green skin and prominent lenticels. Its crisp, juicy white flesh is more tart than sweet, and good for both fresh eating and cooking. It stores well.

Old Field is from Connecticut and referenced in the 1840s, but is probably much older. It is conical, with yellow skin and a red blush. Its cream-colored flesh has a mildly tart flavor.

◀ **Old Nonesuch of Massachusetts** (Bristol, Red Canada) is probably from New England, according to Beach. It dates back to the early 1800s, although its origins are unclear. A round red apple with a green blush and prominent lenticels, it is crisp, juicy, and has outstanding sweet-tart flavor.

◀ **Olive** is a small, round red apple from North Carolina, first cited in the 1860s. Olive was once grown in central Massachusetts. It is crisp, juicy, with outstanding sweet, spicy flavor. William Coxe described another Olive in 1817, a late-season, yellow-green apple with russeting, and yellow flesh, from England, but he does not give its appearance or flavor high grades.

Olive from Vermont was first referenced in 1860, and it is distinct from the variety named Olive from North Carolina.

Orange Sweet, a name shared by apple varieties in Maine, Massachusetts, and Ohio, was first cited in 1835. The Massachusetts Orange Sweet is yellow-green, oblate, and sweet; the Maine apple is also sweet, but rounder in shape and bright yellow. The name Orange Sweet was sometimes applied to two other apples in this list: Golden Sweet, and Munson Sweet.

Ornes Early is an unnamed import to Massachusetts from France. It was described by Charles Mason Hovey under this name around 1850. It is a large yellow apple with a red blush, and its flesh is crisp and juicy.

◀ **Ortley** (White Detroit, Vandyne, White Bellflower, Woolman's Long Pippin) is a New Jersey apple introduced in 1825. Ortley has patches of red on a pale yellow skin. Its dense flesh is a little dry and astringent. The fruit bruises easily, and the trees are susceptible to pests.

▶ **Paragon** is a Winesap-type apple that originated in Tennessee around 1830. It is medium-size, round, ruby red with some russeting, and occasional patches of green. Its texture is crisp but a little dry, and the tough skin partially obscures its mild citrus flavor. It is rare in the North, as it does not grow reliably in colder climes.

Parson was discovered near Springfield, Massachusetts, sometime before 1880. It is a large, dark red apple with outstanding flavor. Its crisp white flesh is sweet and juicy.

▶ **Paw Paw** was named for Paw Paw, Michigan, where it was discovered in the mid-1800s. Dark red with prominent lenticels and a little russeting, its yellow flesh is crisp, moderately juicy, and mostly sweet in flavor, with a hint of tartness. It is a good keeper.

Pease was discovered by Walter Pease in Somers, Connecticut, in the early 1800s. It was once grown in Connecticut's only Shaker community in nearby Enfield. A green-yellow apple with red patches, Pease is crisp, juicy, and mildly sweet in flavor. It bruises easily.

▶ **Peck Pleasant** (Peck) originated in Rhode Island in the early 1800s, and for some years it was widely grown in northern Connecticut. A green, medium-size apple with a pink blush, its flesh is juicy and crisp, and it has a lightly tart flavor, with hints of mango. Its trees are susceptible to disease and often bear small crops. Still, it was once "one of the most salable apples in the market of Providence," wrote Kenrick, and received high praise from Hedrick: "The many spreading, lichen-covered ancients of this old sort to be found in the dooryards and farm orchards of New York and New England are testimonials to the esteem in which lovers of fruit hold it."

◀ **Pewaukee** is a cross of Duchess of Oldenburg and Northern Spy, developed in Pewaukee, Wisconsin, before 1870. A medium-size to large, oblate apple, it is yellow-green with a red blush or stripes and a deep bloom. Its skin is thick, but its flesh is crisp and its sweet flavor has hints of vanilla.

Pickman (Pickman Pippin) was discovered by a Mr. Ware near Salem, Massachusetts, and first described around 1850. It is orange-red with some russeting, and it has cream-colored flesh and tart flavor. It is mostly good for cooking.

Pownal Spitzenburg's name combines its place of origin—Pownal, Vermont—and its resemblance to Esopus Spitzenburg. It dates back to at least the 1840s. It is a large, red, conical apple with dense flesh and a rich, sweet-tart flavor.

President originated in Essex County, Massachusetts, sometime before 1850. It is a large, round apple with pale yellow skin and brown lenticels. Its yellow flesh is crisp, juicy, and sweet-tart.

Priest's Sweet (Blue Sweet, Molasses Sweet) came from Leominster, Massachusetts, prior to 1850. Slightly conical, it is yellow with red stripes and lenticels. Its white flesh is not very juicy, but the apple stores well.

▶ **Primate** was discovered in Onondaga County, New York, in 1840. It is a large yellow apple with a boxy shape; its soft, sweet flesh is yellow.

Progress is from Connecticut, pre-1850. A yellow apple with green patches or brown russeting, it has a pleasant, sweet-tart flavor.

Prolific Sweet came from Connecticut, 1840s or earlier. Conical and green in color, its white flesh has a sweet, spicy flavor best used in cooking.

▶ **Pumpkin Russet** (Pumpkin Sweet, Pumpkin Sweeting, Sweet Russet) was grown in New England beginning in the early 1800s, and first described in 1832. This yellow, russeted apple is bland and sweet, good mostly for cooking.

▶ **Quince of Cole** (Cole's Quince) is an early-season apple discovered by Captain Henry Cole in Cornish, Maine, in the mid-1800s. A medium-size, yellow apple with a boxy shape, it has white flesh and a citrusy sweet-tart flavor that mellows in storage to a quincelike flavor.

◀ **Ralls** is from Virginia, dating to the late 1700s. A large, conical apple, it is mostly red with green highlights. Its flesh is crisp but a little dry, its flavor mildly sweet. It is a good keeper.

◀ **Ramsdell Sweet** (Hurlbut, Ramsdell's Red, Red Pumpkin Sweet) was discovered by Rev. Hezekiah S. Ramsdell (or Ramsdel) of West Thompson, Connecticut, around 1838. It is small, conical, and mostly wine red in color, and its tender flesh is mildly sweet. Early reviews of this apple were decidedly mixed. Kenrick wrote that it was a "prodigious" bearer, and some "have set out whole orchards of this fruit for swine, so great is its productiveness." Hedrick asserted that the trees did not produce large enough crops to be commercially successful.

◀ **Red June** is an early-season apple discovered in North Carolina before 1800, and first described in 1848. It is small, round, and red apple with yellow highlights. Its tender white flesh is juicy, with flavor that is more tart than sweet.

Red Russet originated on a sport of a Baldwin tree on the farm of Aaron Sanborn in Hampton Falls, New Hampshire, around 1840.

Red Seek-No-Further is a Rhode Island fruit, large, and slightly conical. A late-season apple, it is deep red in color with sweet flavor and a little tartness. It is a good keeper.

Rhode Island Russet (Perry Russet) is believed to have originated in Rhode Island sometime before 1850. It is a good all-purpose apple, crisp with a spicy flavor (one early reviewer wrote, "Too many cannot be had, as it is the best of all the Russets"), but it does not store well.

Richardson was discovered by Ebenezer Richardson in Massachusetts, sometime before 1850. A large red apple, it has juicy, greenish white flesh, and it is very sweet.

Rock originated in Peterborough, New Hampshire, and was introduced by Robert Wilson of Keene in the 1840s. A large apple with red stripes and patches over yellow, it has juicy white flesh and sweet-tart flavor.

Rock Sweet was discovered by Elihu Pearson in Newbury, Massachusetts, before 1850. Oblate to conical in shape, its rich red skin has prominent white lenticels. Its crisp, juicy, white flesh is sweet.

Rockport Sweet is a Massachusetts native dating back to the 1840s. It is oblate, green to yellow in color with a red blush. Its white flesh is aromatic and juicy, and its flavor sweet and lively.

Rolfe (Macomber) was once popular in Maine, where it originated around 1820 in the town of Guilford. It may be a seedling of Blue Pearmain. Its flavor is bland, but its trees are hardy.

Rusty Coat was sometimes used to describe any russet apple, particularly in the South. But it was a distinct variety, too, according to Clarence Albert Day in *A History of Maine Agriculture, 1604–1860*, who called it "a delicious little apple, shaped like a strawberry, rather dry."

Rum was discovered by Brownley Rum on his farm in Pawlet, Vermont, prior to 1850. Oblate, it has yellow skin with red highlights. Its flesh is white and juicy, and it has a pleasant, sweet-tart flavor.

▶ **Saint Lawrence** is a large apple dating to at least the early 1800s, with red streaking over a yellow-green skin. Its white flesh is sometimes tinged pink, and it is crisp and juicy. Its mildly tart flavor is best for fresh eating. Vermont pomologist Frank A. Waugh wrote in 1901 that Saint Lawrence was "rather common but not highly prized" in Grand Isle county.

◀ **Salome** was discovered in Ottawa, Illinois, in 1853. It is medium-size, round, with a rich ruby red skin and prominent lenticels. Its flesh is crisp and juicy, and it has outstanding, well-balanced flavor.

Saxton is an old New England variety dating back to at least 1860. It is yellow with patches of red.

Scott Winter (Scott's Red Winter, Scott) originated on the Scott farm in Newport, Vermont, around 1864. Scott Winter experienced some success as a commercial apple in New England in the late 1800s because of the hardiness and reliability of its trees. Its flesh is coarse and it is mild in flavor, but it is a good keeper.

◀ **Seaconk Sweeting** is a midseason apple from Connecticut, dating back to the 1860s. It has watery red streaks over a green skin, similar to Gravenstein. Its flesh is crisp and moderately juicy, and it has a mild, sweet flavor with hints of pear.

◀ **Sheppard's Sweet** is from Windham County, Connecticut, in the mid-1800s. It is large, pink-orange in color with a light yellow blush. It has white flesh and a sweet, pearlike flavor.

▶ **Shiawassee** is from Shiawassee County, Michigan, discovered in 1850. It is oblate in shape, red with some yellow-green and dark red streaks. Its medium crisp flesh is juicy, and it has a sweet, spicy flavor. It was described as being similar but inferior to McIntosh for its strong aroma, juiciness, and sweet-tart flavor.

Smalley (Spice) came from Kensington, Connecticut, "where it was much esteemed," wrote Downing in 1845. It is oblate, medium-size, and yellow with a pink blush. Its flesh is aromatic and juicy, with a pleasing, sweet-tart flavor.

▶ **Somerset of Maine** was discovered in Mercer, Somerset County, Maine, before 1850. A large, oblate, early-season apple, it has yellow skin with red blush or stripes. Its flesh is crisp and juicy, and it has outstanding sweet-tart taste.

Sops of Wine (Bennington, Early Washington) is an early-season apple from England, first cited in 1688. It is a medium-size, oblate, red apple with a yellow-green or reddish purple blush. Its aromatic, tender flesh is white with a pink wash, which probably lends it its name. It has complex flavor, sweet-tart and citrusy, and it is a good cooking and cider apple.

Sparhawk (Gall) is from Walpole, New Hampshire, pre-1850 (by some accounts, it originated in Massachusetts). A large yellow apple with red stripes, it is considered good for cooking and it stores well.

Spice Sweet was discovered on the farm of a Mr. Spurr in Taunton, Massachusetts, before 1820. It is, as its name implies, a sweet, spicy apple.

◀ **Stark** is from Ohio in the mid-1800s. Medium-size, it is red with green patches. Its flesh is crisp and juicy, and it has a nicely balanced sweet-tart flavor.

Starkey was discovered on the farm of Moses Starkey in North Vassalboro, Maine, and first cited in 1875. It has yellow skin with red streaks, and it is a good all-purpose apple.

Steel's Sweet originated in Kensington, Connecticut, prior to 1850. Medium-size and boxy, it is yellow with a pink blush. Its white flesh is dense and juicy, with an oddly sweet flavor.

Stevens's Gilliflower is a large, round to conical apple discovered before 1850 by Mrs. Olive Stevens of Sweden, Maine, pale yellow with red stripes, crisp white flesh, and sweet-tart flavor.

◀ **Stone** originated in Bethel, Vermont, and was cultivated in St. Lawrence County, New York, beginning in 1836 or 1837 by a Mr. Stone. Ruby red with splashes of yellow-green, it is crisp and mildly sweet with a tough skin.

◀ **Summer Pearmain** dates back to the late 1700s. A small, conical, early-season apple, pinkish red over beige, its tender flesh is very juicy and mildly sweet.

Summer Sweet is an old Connecticut apple, pre-1850. It is yellow, with sweet flavor.

Superb Sweet is from Jacob Dean of Mansfield, Massachusetts, cited in 1845. It is pale yellow and red with stripes. A late-season apple once popular in Maine, it has crisp, juicy, white flesh, and rich sweet flavor.

▶ **Sutton** (Morris Red, Sutton Beauty) was named for Sutton, Massachusetts, where it was discovered in the early 1800s. A medium-size apple, rich red in color with patches of green, it is crisp and juicy, and its outstanding sweet flavor has hints of vanilla. According to Beach, Sutton may be a seedling of Hubbardston Nonesuch. The trees are considered difficult to grow.

▶ **Swaar** was developed by Dutch settlers in New York's Hudson River Valley and was first cited in 1804 (its Dutch name refers to its size and weight). It is a large, slightly conical green apple with a yellow blush and some russeting. Its light yellow flesh is crisp, sweet, and moderately juicy. Swaar is considered better for fresh eating than cooking.

Sweet Russet was introduced by Mr. Lyman of Mansfield, Connecticut, and referenced in 1869. It is a medium-size apple with heavy russeting across a yellow skin. It has a rich, spicy sweet flavor, stores well, and is best used in cooking.

Table Greening came from Cornish, Maine, before 1850. Medium-size with a mild, sweet flavor, it stores well.

Tinmouth was discovered in Tinmouth, Vermont, pre-1850. It is a medium-size to large, yellow-green apple with some russeting. Its white flesh is juicy, and it has a "peculiar" sweet-tart flavor, writes Beach.

◀ **Titus Pippin** is from Hempstead, Long Island, New York, in the early 1800s. It is a large, conical, yellow apple with green accents. Moderately crisp and not very juicy, it is a mostly sweet apple.

Tobias was discovered by James Tobias in Grand Isle County, Vermont, before 1890. It is a small, yellow apple of average quality.

Tobias Black was also discovered by James Tobias, before 1890. Dull red-green in color, it has a bland, undistinguished flavor.

Tufts (Tufts Baldwin, Tufts Seedling) originated in Cambridge, Massachusetts, about 1830. It is Baldwin-like in appearance, but has a milder flavor.

Turkey Greening came from Connecticut before 1850. It is large and oblate, with green skin and a dull red blush, and prominent white lenticels. Its flesh is greenish white and juicy, and its sweet-tart flavor mild.

Twitchell's Sweet is from Dublin, New Hampshire, and referenced in the 1840s. Medium-size and conical, it has reddish purple skin with gray lenticels. Its white flesh has red veins, and its flavor is very sweet.

Tydeman's Early Worcester was developed at the Malling Research Station in Kent, England, in 1929, and released commercially in 1945. A cross between McIntosh and Worcester Pearmain, it is a medium-size, round apple, with dark red streaks covering a thin, yellow skin, and prominent white lenticels. Its tender, white flesh combines Worcester Pearmain's strawberry-like flavor with McIntosh's aroma and juiciness. An early-season apple, it is best eaten fresh, and it does not store well.

▶ **Utter** was discovered in Wisconsin and first cited in 1855. It is a medium-size, oblate apple with red streaks on a yellow skin. Its cream-colored flesh is crisp, moderately juicy, and sweet with a little tartness. It is a late-season apple.

▶ **Vandevere** was discovered in Wilmington, Delaware, sometime before 1806. It is a round, late-season apple, green with red patches or stripes. Its yellow flesh is crisp and juicy, its flavor mostly sweet. It is primarily a cooking apple.

Washington Royal (Palmer Greening) originated on the farm of Joseph P. Hayward in Sterling, Massachusetts, and was grown by Ephraim Robbins of nearby Leominster in 1855. It is oblate with waxy, yellow-green skin and a peach-colored blush and juicy flesh, but its flavor is too mild to distinguish it.

▶ **Washington Greening** is of unknown origin, but is still found growing at Tower Hill Botanic Garden, in Boylston, Massachusetts. A medium-size yellow-green apple with a pink blush, its tender flesh is moderately juicy and sweet.

◀ **Washington Strawberry** was discovered in Washington County, New York, in the 1840s. It is a large, beautiful apple, round, red with yellow highlights. It has crisp, cream-colored flesh, and it is moderately juicy. It has a lightly tart flavor with hints of citrus, but it is too mild to be distinguished.

Weston came from the farm of Major Weston in Lincoln, Massachusetts, and was first cited in the 1840s. It is a medium-size, conical apple, with pale yellow skin striped red. Its white flesh is moderately juicy, its flavor mild.

◀ **White Pippin**'s origin is unknown, but it dates to the early 1800s, and it was once widely grown in parts of the Midwest. A round, medium-size to large, yellow-green apple with a pink blush, it has crisp white flesh, is juicy, and has nicely balanced flavor, with hints of citrus and vanilla.

White Sweet came from Maine sometime before 1850. It is a medium-size, round apple, with light yellow skin and a red blush. Its dense flesh is white and juicy, and its flavor very sweet.

Williams (Lady's Apple, Queen, Williams Early, Williams Red) was discovered on the farm of Major Benjamin Williams of Roxbury, Massachusetts, around 1750. It has a rich, deep red color, but its flavor is sweet and bland. It is too mild for cooking, and it does not ship or keep well. Still, Williams enjoyed a measure of popularity in New England and the Mid-Atlantic until about 1900.

Willis's Russet originated in Sudbury, Massachusetts, and was referenced as early as 1845. It is a small, conical apple, with heavy russeting over a yellow skin, and a pink-orange blush. Its flesh is juicy, and it has a sweet, pearlike flavor.

Win Russet is a large, oblate russeted apple with crisp flesh and sweet tart flavor. It was discovered on the farm of John Win in Sweden, Maine, pre-1850.

▶ **Winter Pearmain** was first grown in the 1600s in Plymouth County, Massachusetts. A small to medium-size round, apple, it is lime green with a pink blush. Crisp, juicy, and sweet, its skin is a little chewy. It is considered good for all uses.

▶ **Winthrop Greening** was discovered by Ichabod Howe in Winthrop, Maine, prior to 1800. It is a large, early-season, oblate apple, yellow-green with patches of orange-pink and some russeting. It is crispy, and its flavor is mostly sweet.

Winthrop Pearmain is also from Winthrop, Maine, pre-1850. It is large and round, mostly red over a yellow skin. Its white flesh is juicy, and it has a spicy flavor.

Wood's Sweet (Hyde's Sweet) is a midseason apple from Vermont first cited in 1845, discovered by David Wood Sudbery and introduced by J. M. Ketchum of Brandon. A large, pale yellow apple with sweet flavor, it has crisp, white flesh.

▶ **Wright** is from Hubbardton, Vermont, in the early 1800s. It is a large apple, pink to bright red with yellow highlights. Its crisp white flesh has outstanding flavor, lightly tart with hints of citrus.

The view from the University of Massachusetts Cold Spring Orchard,
Belchertown, Massachusetts.

Acknowledgments

I wish to thank the many apple growers and industry leaders who shared their experiences with me: in Connecticut, John "Jack" Lyman Jr. of Lyman Orchards in Middlefield; in Maine, Manley Brackett of Brackett's Orchards in Limington, and Donald Ricker of Ricker Hill Orchards in Turner; and in Massachusetts David Chandler Sr. of Meadowbrook Orchards in Sterling, William Lord, retired fruit specialist at the University of Massachusetts Extension in Amherst, Edward O'Neill of J. P. Sullivan and Co. in Ayer, William Rose of Red Apple Farm in Phillipston, and Robert Tuttle of Breezelands Orchards in Warren. My mother, Sally Boyce Powell, shared her childhood experiences of the orchard at Elm Hill Farm in Brookfield, where she was born and raised.

In New Hampshire, thanks to Robert Lievens of Woodmont Orchards, and Andy Mack Sr. of Mack's Apples, both in Londonderry, and Eleanor Whittemore of Brookdale Fruit Farm in Hollis; in Rhode Island, James Dame of Dame Farm and Orchards in Johnston, and George Smith of Christiansen's Orchards in Slatersville; and in Vermont, Ray Allen of Allenholm Farm, and Ron and Celia Hackett of Hackett's Orchard, both in South Hero, Russell Allen of Connecticut Valley Orchard in Westminster, and Robert and Betty Douglas of Douglas Orchards in West Shoreham.

Joanne Vieira, director of horticulture at Tower Hill Botanic Garden in Boylston, Massachusetts, John O'Donnell of Easthampton, Massachusetts, retired marketing representative for New York-New England Apple Institute, and Jeannette Robichaud, reference librarian at Old Sturbridge Village (where I discovered serendipitously that my late uncle, Charles Mason Powell, left an extensive collection of early agricultural books), were very helpful and generous with their time.

I had assistance from several people in the apple industry, including Phil Baugher, president of Adams County Nursery, David Bedford, director of the apple-breeding program at the University of Minnesota, John Bunker of Fedco Trees in Waterville, Maine, Frank Carlson of Carlson Orchards in Harvard, Massachusetts, Heather Faubert, University of Rhode Island Extension fruit specialist,

Gary R. Keough, state statistician for the USDA National Agricultural Statistics Service New England Field Office, and Steven Lacasse of Fresh Appeal, former director of the Shoreham Cooperative Apple Producers Association in Vermont.

I wish to thank Kermit Hummel, editorial director, and Lisa Sacks, managing editor, at The Countryman Press, for offering guidance when it was needed and a light hand otherwise. Chris Weeks did an outstanding job preparing the photographs for publication, and I am grateful to Bob Fennelly for providing helpful feedback after reading the manuscript.

I dedicate this book to my collaborator, photographer Bar Lois Weeks, a fastidious and thoughtful editor whose love of the apple rivals mine. In many ways this is the fruit of both our labor.

Bibliography
BOOKS & PERIODICALS

Ahlstrom, Sydney E. *A Religious History of the American People.* New Haven, CT: Yale University Press, 1972.

The Annual Report Golden Anniversary Issue: The First 100 Years, Maine State Pomological Society, 1973.

Annual Report of the Secretary of the Massachusetts State Board of Agriculture, 1900. Boston: Wright & Potter, 1901.

Beach, S. A. *The Apples of New York.* Vols. 1 and 2. Albany: J. B. Lyon Co., 1905.

Branch, Michael P. *Reading the Roots: American Nature Writing Before Walden.* Athens, Georgia: University of Georgia Press, 2004.

Brooks, Reid Merrifield, and Harold Paul Olmo. *Register of New Fruit and Nut Varieties, 1920–1950.* Berkeley, CA: University of California Press, 1952.

Brown, Susan K., and others. *A Catalog of New and Noteworthy Fruits, 1989–1990.* Geneva, New York.

Calhoun, Creighton Lee Jr. *Old Southern Apples.* White River Junction, VT: Chelsea Green, 2010.

Christopher, Everett Percy. "Pomology in Rhode Island," letter to the University of Rhode Island, 1970.

Clark, George F. History of the Temperance Reform in Massachusetts, 1813–1883. Boston: Clarke and Carruth, 1888.

Cole, S. W. *The American Fruit Book.* Boston: John P. Jewett, 1849.

Coxe, William. *A View of the Cultivation of Fruit Trees, and the Management of Orchards and Cider.* Philadelphia: M. Carey and Son, 1817.

Day, Clarence Albert. *A History of Maine Agriculture, 1604–1860.* Orono, ME: University of Maine Press, 1954.

Dirlam, Kenneth H. *John Chapman: By Occupation A Gatherer and Planter of Appleseeds.* Mansfield, OH: Richland County Historical Society, 1953.

Downing, A. J. *Fruits and Fruit Trees of America.* New York: Wiley and Putnam, 1845.

Elliott, F. R. *Elliott's Fruit Book.* New York: C. M. Saxton, 1854.

Gough, Robert E. "Apples from Rhode Island," *University of Rhode Island Cooperative Extension Bulletin.* Kingston: University of Rhode Island, 1978.

Governors of the New England states. *Proceedings of the 1st New England conference called by the Governors of the New England states, Boston, Nov. 23–24, 1908.* Boston: Wright and Potter, 1908.

Griffith, Jeannie. "Fruits of Knowledge," *Cornell University College of Agriculture and Life Sciences News,* Spring 2008.

Haley, William D'Arcy. "Johnny Appleseed, A Pioneer Hero," *Harper's New Monthly Magazine,* November 1871.

Harris, Robert C. *Johnny Appleseed Source Book.* Fort Wayne, Indiana: Public Library of Fort Wayne and Allen County, 1949.

Hedrick, U. P. *A History of Horticulture in America to 1860.* Oxford, England: Oxford University Press, 1950.

_____, *Cyclopedia of Hardy Fruits.* New York: MacMillan, 1922.

Hovey, Charles Mason. *The Fruits of America.* Boston: Hovey and Co., 1852.

Ives, John M. *The New England Book of Fruits.* Salem, MA: W. and S. B. Ives, 1847.

Jones, William Ellery. *Johnny Appleseed: A Voice in the Wilderness.* West Chester, PA: Chrysalis Books, 2000.

Josselyn, John. *An Account of Two Voyages to New England: Made During the Years 1638, 1663.* Boston: W. Veazie, 1865.

Kenrick, William. *The New American Orchardist* (second edition). Boston: Otis, Broaders and Company, 1833.

Kerrigan, William. *Johnny Appleseed and the American Orchard.* Baltimore: Johns Hopkins University Press, 2012.

Lincklaen, John. *Travels in the Years 1791 and 1792 in Pennsylvania, New Jersey, and Vermont.* New York: G. P. Putnam's Sons, 1897.

Manning, Robert. *The New England Fruit Book.* Boston: B. B. Mussey, 1844.

Means, Howard. *Johnny Appleseed: The Man, the Myth, the American Story.* New York: Simon and Schuster, 2011.

Mikolajski, Andrew. *The Illustrated World Encyclopedia of Apples.* Leicestershire, England: Lorenz Books, 2012.

Morgan, Joan, and Alison Richards. *The New Book of Apples.* Rev. ed. London: Ebury Press, 2002.

Munson, W. A., and others. "The Apple Situation in New England," *University of Rhode Island Extension Service Bulletin,* June 1928.

Munson, W. A. "Preliminary Notes on the Seedling Apples of Maine," *Annual Report of the Maine Agricultural Experiment Station, Bulletin 115.* Orono, ME, 1907.

Nason, Fayre. "Stearns Lothrop Davenport," letter to the Worcester County Horticultural Society (nd).

Pollan, Michael. *The Botany of Desire.* New York: Random House, 2002.

Powell, R. S. *America's Apple.* Hatfield, MA: Brook Hollow Press. 2012.

Price, Robert. *Johnny Appleseed: Man & Myth.* Urbana, OH: Urbana University, 1954.

Russell, Howard S. *A Long, Deep Furrow: Three Centuries of Farming in New England.* Abridged ed. Hanover, NH: University of New England Press, 1982.

Sanders, Rosie. *The Apple Book.* London: Frances Lincoln, 2010.

Sayers, Edward. *The American Fruit Garden Companion.* Boston: Weeks, Jordan and Co., 1839.

Smock, R. M. and A. M. Neubert. *Apples and Apple Products.* New York: Interscience Publishers, 1950.

Stilphen, George. *The Apples of Maine.* 2nd ed. Otisfield, ME: self-published, 2000.

Taylor, Charles E. *History of Great Barrington (Berkshire County), Massachusetts.* Great Barrington, MA: C. W. Bryan and Co., 1882.

Teskey, Benjamin J. E., and James S. Shoemaker. *Tree Fruit Production.* Second edition. Westport, CT: Avi Publishing, 1972.

Thacher, James. *The American Orchardist.* Boston: J. W. Ingraham, 1825.

Thomas, John J. *The American Fruit Culturist.* New York: W. Wood and Company, 1897.

Thoreau, Henry David. *Cape Cod.* Boston: Ticknor & Fields, 1865.

_____. *Walden (Or Life in the Woods).* Radford, VA: Wilder Publications, 2008.

_____. "Wild Apples," *The Writings of Henry David Thoreau.* Boston: Houghton Mifflin Co., 1906.

Warder, John Ashton. *American Pomology: Apples.* New York: Orange Judd, 1867.

Waugh, Frank Albert, "Apple Growing in Addison County," *Vermont Agricultural Experiment Station Bulletin No. 90*, December 1901.

_____. "Apple Growing in Grand Isle County," *Vermont Agricultural Experiment Station Bulletin No. 55*, December 1896.

_____. "Hardy Apples for Cold Climates," *Vermont Agricultural Experiment Station Bulletin No. 61*, November 1897.

_____. *The American Apple Orchard.* New York: Orange Judd, 1908.

Way, Roger D., and others. *A Catalog of New and Noteworthy Fruits, 1971–1972.* Geneva, NY.

Way, Roger D., and others. *A Catalog of New and Noteworthy Fruits, 1976–1977.* Geneva, NY.

Way, Roger D. "Apple Cultivars Introduced by the New York State Agricultural Experiment Station, 1914–1968," *Search Agriculture* 1, no. 2. Ithaca, NY: Cornell University, 1971.

Whitney, Peter. *History of the County of Worcester.* Worcester, MA: Isaiah Thomas, 1793.

WEBSITES

Authorship is uncredited and very likely shared on the majority of the websites cited here:

"Apples—History and Legends of Apples," www.whatscookingamerica.net/Fruit/Apples.htm.

"Apple Varieties," Out on a Limb Heritage Apple CSA, www.outonalimbcsa.wordpress.com/alexander.

"Connecticut Pomological Society Records," www.doddcenter.uconn.edu/asc/findaids/CT_Pomology/MSS19980347.html.

Forstall, Richard L. "Vermont Population of Counties by Decennial Census: 1900 to 1990." US Bureau of the Census, www.census.gov/population/cencounts/vt190090.txt, 1995.

"Historic Tree Stories," American Forests, www.americanforests.org/our-programs/historic-trees/historic-tree-stories/.

"History of Old Orchard Beach," Maine Resource Guide, www.maineguide.com/region/southcoast/information/oobhistory.html.

"Honeybees and Colony Collapse Disorder," United States Department of Agriculture Research Service, www.ars.usda.gov/news/docs.htm?docid=15572.

"Of Horticulture and Antislavery: The Kenricks of Newton," Brighton-Allston Historical Society, www.bahistory.org.

"Ontario Ministry of Agriculture and Food," www.omafra.gov.on.ca/english/index.html.

"Trees of Antiquity," www.treesofantiquity.com.

"University of Minnesota Apples," www.apples.umn.edu.

Vermont Farmer, vtdnp.wordpress.com/2011/02/, Vermont Digital Newspaper Project weblog, February 7, 2011.

"The Great Hurricane of 1938," www.bigstory.ap.org/article/ap-photos-great-new-england-hurricane-1938.

The Vermont Farmer, www.chroniclingamerica.loc.gov/lccn/sn84023255/.

Witherell Elizabeth, and Elizabeth Dubrulle. "The Writings of Henry David Thoreau," thoreau.library.ucsb.edu/thoreau_life.html.

Resources

American Pomological Society

www.americanpomological.org

Connecticut Apple Marketing Board

www.ctapples.com

860-713-2503

Fedco Trees

www.fedcoseeds.com/trees.htm

P.O. Box 520, Waterville, ME 04903

207-426-9900

Maine State Pomological Society

www.maineapples.org

c/o Highmoor Farm,

P.O. Box 179, Monmouth, ME 04259

207-933-2100

Massachusetts Fruit Growers Association

www.massfruitgrowers.org

New England Apple Association

www.newenglandapples.org

P.O. Box 41, Hatfield, MA 01038

203-439-7006

Rhode Island Fruit Growers Association

www.rifruitgrowers.org

Tower Hill Botanic Garden

www.towerhillbg.org

11 French Drive, Boylston, MA 01505-0598

508-869-6111

United States Apple Association

www.usapple.org

8233 Old Courthouse Rd, Suite 200,

Vienna, VA 22182

703-442-8850

Vermont Tree Fruit Growers Association

www.vermontapples.org

Index